RECALIBRATE YOUR SELF-WORTH

JEN TRAVERSE

Published by Prominence Publishing. www.Prominencepublishing.com

Recalibrate Your Self-Worth / Jen Traverse. -- 1st ed.

ISBN: 978-1-997649-13-7

Dedication

Lena and Lucas,

This book is dedicated to you, the brightest stars in my universe. May you always find the magic, love, and satisfaction you desire, no matter where life's journey takes you. Remember, the universe has a way of weaving its wonders and winking at you to make sure you know that everything happens for a reason.

If life ever leads you down a path where you seek more, imagine it vividly. Dream big and paint the most colorful images in your mind, for that is what you will manifest. Trust in the magic of the universe and the power within to create your own destiny.

I love you forever and ever, Always, Always, Always, No matter what happens.

Love Mama

Table of Contents

Table of Contents

Introduction

"You, yourself, as much as anybody in the entire universe, deserve your love and affection."
Buddha

Living in the Philadelphia area, I had always thrived on order. My role at work meant my days were filled with schedules, deadlines, and meticulously charted to-do lists created by someone else. My talent for organizing and planning was both admired and envied, but beneath my polished exterior, there was a whispering urge for something more meaningful and spontaneous.

One evening, while flipping through channels in the small apartment I shared, I stumbled upon a documentary about the vibrant city life and natural beauty of Seattle. My brother had been living there for a few years and although I had been there to visit, I had never thought about moving there until this moment. The sheer thrill and unpredictability of the city struck a chord deep within me. I realized I had been craving an adventure, something that would push me beyond my comfort zone. In a decision that surprised everyone, including myself, I decided to take a break from my career and move to Seattle.

INTRODUCTION

I packed my bags which included a hockey bag and a hiking pack, and left behind the structured world I had created. This was my first big move by myself, and it felt liberating yet daunting. My initial days in Seattle were anything but graceful. Used to controlling my environment, the city's unpredictability was a bit overwhelming. Each day felt like trying to navigate a new landscape with a map drawn by a child.

But with each stumble, I learned something new. Slowly, I began to appreciate the moments of stillness amid the city's bustle, the rhythm of the vibrant culture, and the thrill of discovering each new neighborhood. I discovered that letting go of control was therapeutic. The challenges I once feared became my teachers, showing me resilience and the ease I had been searching for.

My time in Seattle transformed my understanding of life. The chaos I once avoided became a source of strength, teaching me that the most defining moments come from daring to dive headfirst into the unknown. From then on, I continued to build upon the foundation of courage and eagerness for the unknown I had created in Seattle and found myself ready for whatever life might bring next. It was this very spirit of resilience and adaptability that inspired me to share my journey and insights with others. This book isn't just a guide; it's your lifeline for navigating those moments with a blend of ease, confidence, and grace. Trust me, you're not alone in this shitshow. We've all been there, and we're in it together, riding the highs and lows, learning to Recalibrate our lives for the better. Because it is when we learn this flow, we finally Recalibrate our worthiness.

When I first set out to write this book, I had this grand vision of handing out practical tools like candy, helping folks manage life's pivotal moments with surgical precision. But life, as it tends to do, threw me a curveball. As

RECALIBRATE YOUR SELF-WORTH

I sifted through my past, I uncovered a recurring theme: the stories that shaped me often left me feeling like shit; empty, low, and questioning everything. These narratives forced me to scrutinize the traditions I clung to and the decisions I thought were mine.

Unraveling these layers, I realized that understanding how our beliefs about success and self-worth evolve and weave together is crucial. I started mapping my life like some kind of existential treasure hunt, drawing lines between past fuck-ups and current realities, trying to figure out why certain moments unfolded the way they did. Recalibrating your self-worth is about stepping back, evaluating our choices, and Recalibrating for a future that not only looks satisfying but feels damn good, too.

Scribbling about goals and achievements while drowning in dread and isolation is a paradox that many people experience but few openly discuss during this evaluation. Feeling of unworthiness is tied to the unsettling feeling that, despite outward success, something is profoundly missing. You find yourself ticking off boxes on a list that society, family, or even your past self has handed you, yet each tick feels hollow. You begin to question, "Is this it?" This question that haunts you in quiet moments, nags at you during your daily routine, and wakes you up at night. This is the point where I found myself, caught in a cycle of meeting expectations that weren't truly mine, feeling emotionally and spiritually stagnant.

Outwardly, my life seemed successful. I had a career that others envied, a family that was happy and healthy, and a lifestyle that many would consider ideal. Yet, beneath this polished veneer, I was grappling with a deep sense of isolation and a pervasive dread that I couldn't shake off. It was as if I were living someone else's life, adhering to rules and norms that didn't resonate with who I truly was. The achievements that were supposed to bring fulfillment instead felt like chains, binding me to a version of myself that I hadn't consciously chosen.

INTRODUCTION

The turning point came when I realized I needed a bridge; a way to connect the life I lived by others' rules to the one crafted on my terms. This bridge would serve as the foundation for self-worth and acceptance like I never knew before. This bridge would be the reason I finally smiled when I opened the closet that held my skeletons and would be the walkway to the light at the end of the tunnel. This realization was a game-changer. It was like a light bulb flickering on in a dark room, illuminating the path I needed to take. But building this bridge wasn't going to be easy. It required me to confront some hard truths and ask difficult questions about purpose, motherhood, and authenticity.

Purpose became a central theme in this journey. What did I want my life to stand for? What legacy did I want to leave behind? These questions forced me to look beyond the superficial markers of success and delve into what truly mattered to me. I realized that my purpose wasn't just about achieving professional milestones or accumulating material wealth. My purpose, my self-worth, was about making a meaningful impact, both in my personal life and in the broader world. This meant redefining success on my terms, which was both liberating and terrifying.

Motherhood added another layer of complexity to this introspection. As a mother, I was acutely aware of the example I was setting for my children. I wanted them to see a mother who was not only successful but also fulfilled and authentic. This meant I had to model the courage to live authentically, even if it meant making uncomfortable changes. I began to prioritize presence over perfection, focusing on being truly present with my children rather than striving for some unattainable ideal of motherhood. Let me tell you, this was fucking tough given the media impact these days.

RECALIBRATE YOUR SELF-WORTH

Authenticity, then, became another cornerstone of my approach to life. It required unearthing layers of societal expectations and self-imposed limitations to uncover my true self. I had to confront the fear of judgment and the possibility of failure, acknowledging that living authentically might not always be easy, but it was necessary for my well-being. This meant embracing my imperfections and vulnerabilities, recognizing that they were not weaknesses but integral parts of my identity.

The journey to living life on my terms has been both challenging and rewarding. It has involved letting go of the need for external validation and learning to trust my instincts. It has meant saying fuck it to paths that didn't serve me and embracing those that did, even if they were less conventional. This process has been transformative, allowing me to break free from the cycle of dread and isolation and move toward a life of purpose and fulfillment.

In the end, the bridge I built was not just a connection to a new way of living; it was a testament to my resilience and determination. It was the key to Recalibrating my self-worth. It was a reminder that despite the shit life throws at us, we have the power to redefine our paths and create lives that are truly our own. Returning to meditation became my anchor, offering clarity and comfort. It allowed my thoughts to surface and guide me. I realized that sharing my insights, stories, and vulnerabilities wasn't just cathartic for me; it was essential for anyone else feeling similarly lost. This book is my invitation to you to explore your journey, armed with the wisdom and experiences I've gathered.

In the fast-paced and often overwhelming world we live in, the quest for self-discovery and personal growth is a challenge, but a necessity. This book, structured in three distinct phases, serves as your roadmap to navigating this transformative journey of Recalibration. Each phase is designed to guide you deeper into your own being, allowing you to expose the layers of your true self and cultivate a life of purpose and fulfillment.

Phase One: Awakening from Autopilot

In the frenetic pace of contemporary life, many of us find ourselves knee deep in a cycle of routines and habits that operate almost automatically. This autopilot mode of existence, while efficient for managing daily tasks, often results in a life that feels mechanical and devoid of genuine fulfillment. The true essence of living intentionally and purposefully becomes overshadowed by the automatic repetition of our daily activities. This phase, "Awakening from Autopilot," is dedicated to dismantling this unconscious mode of living and guiding you toward a life of greater awareness, intention, and meaning.

Autopilot living is characterized by a lack of conscious awareness in our daily activities. We wake up, go through our morning routine, commute to work, handle our tasks, and return home, only to wash, rinse, and repeat the cycle the next day. This pattern, while seemingly innocuous, can lead to a profound disconnect from our inner selves and the world around us. We may find ourselves questioning, "Is this all there is?" or feeling an inexplicable void despite achieving societal markers of success.

Phase Two: Shifting Perspectives

Once we have shaken off the shackles of autopilot living, the next step is to shift our perspectives. This phase, appropriately named "Shifting Perspectives," involves a profound transformation in how we perceive our circumstances and the bigger picture. It requires a conscious effort to challenge and reframe our existing beliefs and perceptions, which often shape our daily experiences and interactions.

In this phase, you are encouraged to explore new ways of thinking and to question the assumptions that have previously guided your life. This transformative journey is crucial for personal growth and fulfillment, as it opens a world of possibilities that were previously obscured by habitual thought patterns. By adopting a more open and flexible mindset, we can begin to see challenges as opportunities and setbacks as valuable lessons.

Stories of transformation play a vital role in illustrating the power of shifting perspectives. The narratives shared in this book often highlight individuals who have undergone significant changes in their lives by altering their viewpoints. For example, someone who once viewed failure as a definitive end might come to see it as a stepping stone to success. Another person might transform their perspective on adversity, recognizing it as a catalyst for resilience and innovation.

Ultimately, "Shifting Perspectives" is about embracing the idea that change is not only possible but necessary for achieving a deeper sense of meaning, satisfaction, and the worthiness we want to have in life. By actively reshaping our worldview, we can break free from limiting beliefs, enhance our emotional well-being, and create a more fulfilling and purposeful existence.

Phase Three: Daily Recalibration

The final phase, "Daily Recalibration," is about integrating the insights and lessons from our journey into our everyday lives. It involves aligning our actions with our values and aspirations, creating a foundation for authentic living and lasting change. Daily Recalibration requires us to establish rituals and habits that support our well-being and personal growth. These rituals serve as anchors, grounding us in the present moment and reminding us of our intentions. They can include practices such as meditation, reflection, and intentional action.

INTRODUCTION

Use what you read in the book as a guide to navigate the transformative journey of self-discovery and personal growth that lies ahead. Through the phases of Awakening, Shifting Perspectives, and Daily Recalibration, we learn to live more consciously and authentically, creating a life of profound satisfaction, purpose, and fulfillment. This journey is a lifelong adventure, inviting us to continually explore the depths of our being and embrace the boundless potential that lies within us.

I want you to finish this book having a fresh vantage point that empowers you to evaluate your past, recognize your strengths, and show up more fully in your life with a renewed sense of worthiness and forgiveness for yourself. This journey is about Recalibrating our understanding of self-worth and embracing the freedom and satisfaction that come from truly knowing ourselves. It's about waking up from the autopilot mode that so many of us fall into and taking the wheel of our own lives. Approach this journey with curiosity and openness, knowing that you're here for a reason. Life is a series of moments, some chaotic, some serene, all of them opportunities to learn and grow. Together, let's embark on this path of self-discovery, learning to navigate the twists and turns with grace and grit. Remember, the path to self-discovery isn't a solitary one. We're in this together, learning, growing, and Recalibrating every step of the way.

As we transition to Chapter 1, I will share one of my stories about how, at 45, I found myself at a crossroads. This very personal journey is a testament to the transformative power of Recalibration. My life, marked by both triumphs and trials, had brought me to a pivotal moment of introspection and change. Are you ready to take control and redefine what success and self-worth mean to you? If so, let's fucking go.

Phase 1
Life on Autopilot

CHAPTER 1

Why Now?

"Who looks outside, dreams; who looks inside, awakes."
Carl Jung

At 45, I found myself at a crossroads, staring down the winding paths of my life with a mix of trepidation and curiosity. My once dark, glossy black hair, now peppered with silver, framed a face marked by laugh lines and wisdom that only comes from life's trials and triumphs. This journey to self-awareness and worthiness has been anything but linear, beginning with a pivotal event. My divorce.

The divorce was a monumental shift, overturning the carefully curated life I had presented to the world. It was a period marred by betrayal and disillusionment, where those I considered allies revealed themselves as adversaries. This painful, yet necessary disruption shattered the illusion of my carefully constructed life, forcing me to confront the raw truth of who I was and what I wanted. Even though I knew it was coming, the timeline and speed of which the actual events unfolded was like having the rug pulled out from under me, leaving me with no choice but to face the shitstorm head-on.

WHY NOW?

The year(s) leading up to the divorce, I realized I had been living on autopilot. For years, I was stuck in a cycle of routine and habit, living a life that looked fulfilling from the outside but felt hollow within. My days were filled with mundane tasks, ticking off boxes that society and I had deemed markers of success. Yet, beneath this façade of accomplishment, I felt a growing sense of disconnection. It was both emancipating and terrifying to confront the fact that I had been living according to a script dictated by societal norms and external expectations, rather than my own desires and values.

Amidst the turmoil in those years that followed the divorce, I felt a flicker of hope, a sense that this was an opportunity to rebuild my life on my own terms. It was during the period of upheaval and rebuilding that followed that I began to recognize the strength that had always simmered beneath the surface while I was married. My fears of being an eternal seeker of life's purpose were tempered by a newfound appreciation for the journey itself, rather than the destination.

Awakening from autopilot didn't happen overnight. It started with small, deliberate steps toward living a more conscious and intentional life. I introduced mindfulness practices into my daily routine and turned to journaling to process my thoughts and emotions. Writing became a therapeutic outlet, a means of exploring my inner world and clarifying what truly mattered to me. Through writing, I began to uncover patterns and habits that were holding me back and realized that I had been prioritizing external achievements over my own well-being.

A vivid memory of a recent coffee date with a friend stands out as a turning point. As we sat outside a café, I was struck by the simplicity of the moment: the sun's warmth, the aromatic blend of cinnamon and vanilla in my cup, and my friend's genuine enthusiasm as she spoke of new beginnings. This encounter was a mirror, reflecting my own potential for renewal and growth. Driving home that day, my mind was a whirlwind of introspection. I realized how dramatically my life had shifted since the divorce. My children were growing rapidly, and I was navigating the complexities of single motherhood while maintaining my career. The realization dawned that I was, indeed, recalibrating my life, aligning it with my true self rather than the expectations of others.

This realization became one of the driving forces for this book. I understood that the stories I wanted to share were not just my own but universal narratives of transformation and growth. I wanted those who found this book to find solace and strength in the shared human experience of recalibrating one's life and thus recalibrating one's self-worth. The past holds valuable lessons, but it is the future that beckons with possibilities. That day, as I drove away from the coffee shop, I felt a profound sense of peace. I was ready to embrace the next phase of my life with even more appreciation and openness than I did before. My journey was far from over, but I was no longer on autopilot. I was in the driver's seat, steering toward a future defined by my own terms.

Reflecting on my journey, I recognize how easily we can fall into the trap of autopilot living. Routine becomes a comfort, a way to manage the chaos of daily life. But over time, these routines can calcify, transforming freedom into a cage that limits our ability to live fully and intentionally. As I continued this path, I was reminded that the journey is just as important as the destination. Each step, each choice, and each moment of awareness brings us closer to a life of greater fulfillment and purpose. By integrating research and personal experience, I could model a roadmap for others who are seeking to break free from autopilot and embrace a more intentional and meaningful life. Shifting from autopilot starts with recognizing that we are, in fact, in autopilot.

WHY NOW?

Incorporating mindfulness into daily life was a pivotal step in my journey toward conscious living. Mindfulness involves paying attention to the present moment with openness and curiosity, without judgment. This practice can be integrated into various aspects of life, from mindful eating and walking to more structured practices like meditation and physical activity. Through mindfulness, I learned to observe my thoughts and emotions without getting caught up in them. This awareness allowed me to recognize when I was slipping into autopilot and to gently bring my focus back to the present. It was a gradual process, requiring patience and practice, but the benefits were profound. I found myself more engaged in my interactions, more attuned to my surroundings, and more satisfied with my experiences. The benefits of mindfulness are well-supported by research. A study by Creswell (2017) found that mindfulness can improve psychological well-being, reduce stress, and enhance cognitive flexibility. These findings align with my own experiences, as mindfulness helped me develop a greater sense of resilience and adaptability in the face of life's challenges.

Another powerful tool in my journey was writing. By setting aside time each day to write about my thoughts, feelings, and experiences, I created a space for self-reflection and exploration. Writing helped me identify patterns and habits that were no longer serving me and provided clarity on the changes I needed to make. Research by Pennebaker and Seagal (1999) supports the therapeutic benefits of expressive writing, demonstrating that it can lead to improvements in mental health and well-being. Writing about our experiences allows us to process emotions, gain insight into our behaviors, and develop a clearer understanding of our values and goals. As a visual person, writing helped me clearly see where I had been and provided a way for me to articulate my goals and track my progress over time. This practice not only enhanced my self-awareness but also reinforced my commitment to living intentionally. By documenting my journey, I created a tangible record of my growth and transformation, which served as a source of inspiration and guidance for those who read it.

Although the foundation of this process is self-reflection, breaking free from autopilot is not a journey that we must undertake completely solo. Community and support play a vital role in fostering conscious living. Once we identify our next steps, surrounding ourselves with individuals who share our values and aspirations can provide encouragement and accountability as we navigate the challenges of intentional living. In my own journey, I found strength and inspiration in the communities I have built through my work as a mindset coach and speaker. These connections provided a space for sharing experiences, exchanging ideas, and supporting one another in our pursuit of a more intentional life. Research by Holt-Lunstad et al. (2010) suggests that social support is linked to improved mental health and well-being. This underscores the importance of fostering connections and building a supportive network as we work toward breaking free from autopilot.

To delve deeper into the science behind conscious living, it's essential to explore how our brains function on autopilot and the mechanisms that allow us to break free from this state. The brain's default mode network (DMN) is a network of interacting brain regions that is active when a person is not focused on the outside world. When we are engaged in routine tasks, the DMN allows us to perform them without active thought, conserving cognitive resources for more demanding activities. However, this efficiency can become a trap, leading us to live passively rather than actively engaging with our surroundings. Research by Gouraud, Delorme, and Berberian (2017) discusses how autopilot and mind wandering can lead to an "out of the loop" performance problem, where individuals may feel disconnected from their actions and decisions. This insight was crucial for me when I was evaluating my self-worth related to my previous decisions and outcomes. It emphasized the need to engage more actively with my life choices, ensuring that I was present and intentional in my actions.

Similarly, research by Korponay (2023) highlights the role of the ventrolateral prefrontal cortex in overriding habits in real-time, emphasizing the neurological basis for breaking free from autopilot. Understanding this scientific research helped me further understand my own thought processes and the potential for change through conscious effort. I mean, isn't it fucking great to know how the brain supports our ability to change patterns? With deliberate practice, we can rewire our neural pathways to foster more intentional living. I may sound like I am obsessing about the scientific aspect, but the bottom line is that we have complete control, and it often comes down to whether or not we decide to use it. Siddiquee's (2024) research substantiates how the power of deliberate thinking can directly impact the autopilot mind. This perspective resonated deeply with my journey, as I learned to harness the art of conscious thought to transform my life and achieve my goals. By embracing this mindset, I was able to navigate my path with clarity and purpose, moving away from routine and towards a life of intentional action.

Waking up from the autopilot mode, we often find ourselves realizing that it isn't just a one-time event; it's an ongoing adventure that demands real commitment, a good dose of self-awareness, and a brave heart ready to welcome change. It's about taking a hard look at ourselves and deciding what we really want our lives to stand for, aligning our actions with those values, and carving out a life that's genuinely ours.

RECALIBRATE YOUR SELF-WORTH

When I think about my own journey, I realize I'm not alone. So many of us get trapped in the daily grind, going through the motions without actually being present. It's like we're sleepwalking through life, letting routine and habit take the wheel. But what happens when we decide enough is enough and start setting the bar for what we're willing to accept?

That's where Alicia comes in. Her story is a powerful example of what it means to wake up and shake things up. Alicia decided it was time to stop settling for a life defined by other people's expectations and start living on her own terms. She embarked on a journey of recalibration, raising her standards and embracing her true worth, not based on what others think, but on her own inner compass.

Alicia's transformation is all about appreciating her achievements and recognizing that her value comes from within. This newfound clarity gives her the confidence to live authentically, stepping away from the monotonous routines that once held her back. As we dive into Alicia's story, we find a lesson in courage and authenticity that sets the stage for our next chapter, where we all learn to live a life that truly resonates with our deepest values and desires.

CHAPTER 2: RAISING THE BAR

What's My Minimum Standard?

"Any time you sincerely want to make a change,
the first thing you must do is to raise your standards."
Tony Robbins

In the heart of New Orleans, where the air is thick with jazz and the scent of beignets, Alicia found herself at a pivotal moment in her life. At 38, Alicia was a woman of striking resilience, her bright eyes reflecting a blend of determination and vulnerability. Her straight brown hair framed a face that had weathered both storms of joy and sorrow, and her frame bore the scars of past battles, both physical and emotional.

Alicia's journey was marked by a series of setbacks that had left her questioning her worth and capabilities. A former gymnast, she had been sidelined by a devastating hip injury that required surgery, leaving her mobility severely limited. The pain was a constant companion, a reminder of what she had lost and what she could no longer do. Her once vibrant life felt like a prison, each day a struggle against the confines of her own body.

It was at a TEDx talk in 2021, where she worked behind the scenes, that Alicia's life took an unexpected turn. As she listened to the speaker discuss the power of recalibrating one's life, a flicker of hope that had long been extinguished stirred within her. After the talk, the speaker, intrigued by Alicia's attentive presence, encouraged her to stay in touch. This brief interaction planted a seed of possibility in Alicia's mind, a whisper of change that she couldn't ignore.

In the months that followed, Alicia found herself at a crossroads, a place where the road ahead seemed shrouded in uncertainty and despair. Her doctors had delivered the news with a clinical detachment that left her reeling: Her condition might never improve. It was a gut punch, a stark reminder of the limitations that seemed to define her existence. But deep down, Alicia felt a glint of something more; a stubborn flame of desire that refused to be extinguished. She craved a life beyond the constant pain and the suffocating constraints imposed on her by well-meaning but ultimately disheartening prognoses.

It was during one of those particularly shitty days, when everything felt like it was crashing down and the weight of her despair was almost unbearable, that Alicia made a choice. It was a "fuck-this" moment, a defiant decision to raise her minimum standard and refuse to be defined by her circumstances. Seeking help was her first brave step. She began seeing a counselor, a compassionate guide who could help untangle the web of her past and illuminate a new path forward. In those therapy sessions, Alicia confronted the coping mechanisms she had clung to since childhood, recognizing how they had insidiously shaped her adult life.

The process was raw and emotional. She unearthed memories she had long buried, each revelation a painful but necessary excavation of her soul. Yet, through the tears and the heartache, Alicia began to see her mental health diagnosis not as a shackle, but as a key to understanding herself more deeply than she ever had before. With each breakthrough, she discovered a newfound strength within, a resilience that had been quietly waiting for its moment to shine.

As Alicia Recalibrated her emotional barriers, she began to rebuild her self-esteem, transforming her inner dialogue from one of defeat to one of empowerment. It wasn't an overnight transformation, but a gradual shift, each day bringing her closer to the person she wanted to become. Her physical journey mirrored this emotional metamorphosis. With the support of a dedicated personal trainer, Alicia started to push her boundaries. She began with a mere 200 painful, arduous steps a day. She slowly increased her steps, and as she did, her determination propelled her forward with each stride. Her trainer watched in awe as Alicia transformed before his eyes. There was something magical about witnessing her progress, the way her resolve fueled her, step by step, until one day she found herself walking over 10,000 steps.

It was a triumphant moment, one that brought tears of pride and joy. Alicia wasn't just moving physically; she was moving emotionally and spiritually, breaking free from the chains of her past and forging a new future. With every step, Alicia was not just defying the odds. She was redefining them, proving to herself and the world that she was capable of so much more than anyone had dared to dream. And in those moments of triumph, Alicia realized that the crossroads she had once feared was not an endpoint, but a new beginning.

Alicia's story is one of recalibration, of raising her minimum standard and refusing to accept a life defined by limitations. She learned to appreciate her accomplishments and the journey that had brought her where she was, understanding that her self-worth was not determined by others' expectations, but by her own belief in herself. Her relationships flourished as she embraced open communication with her loved ones, valuing the exchange of feedback as a tool for growth. Alicia also rediscovered her love for art, using it as a creative outlet to express her evolving identity. Her faith, once a dormant thought, was reignited, providing her with a sense of peace and purpose.

The decision to seek help was Alicia's turning point, the moment she decided she was worth more than the life she had been living. By raising her minimum standard, she opened herself to a world of possibilities, allowing her to envision a future where she was not just surviving but truly thriving. Alicia's journey is a testament to the power of self-belief and the courage it takes to demand more from life. She serves as a beacon of hope for anyone standing at their own crossroads, reminding us that change begins with a single decision to raise the bar and embrace the potential within.

In the quiet moments of reflection, Alicia found solace in the teachings of mindfulness and self-compassion. Drawing inspiration from the previous books in the Recalibrate series, *Wirtz* (2020) and *Traverse* (2023), she learned that recalibration is not an endpoint but an ongoing process of aligning one's life with core values and aspirations. This understanding empowered her to navigate life's uncertainties with grace and resilience. Alicia's story invites us to examine our own lives and the standards we set for ourselves. It challenges us to question: What are we willing to accept, and what are we determined to change? By shifting our mindset and embracing the journey of growth, we open ourselves to a future filled with promise and possibility.

Alright, so we've seen Alicia kick ass and redefine what it means to truly live. Now it's time to dive even deeper and tackle the shit that's been holding us back for way too long. Enter Chapter 3, where we're about to break the chains of the bullshit stories and traditions that have been handed down to us like a family heirloom. It's time to ask the tough questions: What stories have we been told, and what expectations have we blindly upheld? As we unravel the layers and complexity of inherited beliefs, we're going to find out what truly resonates with us and what we need to live life on our own fucking terms. Get ready to dig in, because this chapter is all about shedding the old and embracing the freedom to be who we were always meant to be.

CHAPTER 3: BREAKING THE CHAINS

What Stories and Traditions Have I Upheld?

"Your beliefs become your thoughts, your thoughts become your words, your words become your actions, your actions become your habits, your habits become your values, your values become your destiny."

Mahatma Gandhi

"You have to be nice." "You have to maintain good grades." "You should go to college." "You should have a good relationship, get married, and have a family." These were the mantras of my upbringing, passed down like sacred relics from my parents, who in turn received them from theirs. I grew up believing these were the immutable truths of life, as unyielding as the seasons of New England. And for a long time, I tried to mold myself into this template, thinking it was the only way to live a worthy life.

But here's the kicker. I didn't realize until much later that their best might not have been my best. Growing up, I was spoon-fed expectations, told how to live, what to strive for, and who to become. It was like being handed a script for a role I never auditioned for. And let me tell you, playing that part was exhausting as hell. It took a rebellion, a series of painful life lessons, and a hell of a lot of soul-searching to figure that out. I'm talking about the kind of rebellion that doesn't just disrupt your life, it fucking shakes it to the core. Eating disorders, a suicide attempt, severe self-loathing, alcoholism, divorce, and career changes were each its own battle, a desperate attempt to break free from the life I was told to live. I was trying to escape the box I had been put in, even if it meant breaking myself in the process.

Shifting from rebellion to allowance wasn't an instant miracle; it was a slow, laborious trek through the life I had created. Imagine wading through the wreckage of your life, picking up the pieces, and trying to figure out which ones still fit. The tools I used to create this shift are well-documented in the Recalibrate series, a collection of books and workbooks that guided me from the brink of despair to a place of understanding and acceptance. They became my lifeline, helping me navigate through the chaos and find a semblance of peace.

This journey led me to a pivotal question that haunted me: Did I fail my parents because I wasn't the model kid they expected, or have I succeeded in my own life because I broke the mold? It was a question that gnawed at me, keeping me up at night. On the one hand, there was the guilt of not living up to their dreams, of not being the person they envisioned. On the other, there was the exhilarating freedom of carving out my own path, of living a life that felt authentically mine. In the end, I realized that success isn't about meeting someone else's expectations; it's about finding your own truth and living it unapologetically. Sure, my journey was messy, filled with fuck-ups and wrong turns, but it was mine. And in that mess, I found strength, resilience, worthiness, and finally, the courage to be myself. So, while I may not be the poster child my parents imagined, I am the person I was always meant to be. And that, to me, is the real victory.

This question was my North Star, guiding me as I sifted through the traditions and expectations handed down to me. I had to decide which of these were true for who I was and who I wanted to become. I had to ask myself how much freedom I was willing to grant myself and how much of it I could comfortably embrace. It was as daunting as existential questions like "Why am I here?" or "What does it all mean?" I began by examining the beliefs I was trying to disprove. What was the core belief behind these traditions? Alongside a few positive core beliefs, I unearthed a laundry list of negative ones that had seeped into my psyche. These were the beliefs I needed to confront to shift my perspective and bridge the life I was told to lead and the life I chose to create.

Let's start with an easier one: my career. I was told to pick something I liked and make it my career. My generation wasn't coached to accept that preferences change over time. Instead, I felt judged, like a failure for not sticking with one path. In psychology, the phenomenon of feeling like an impostor despite evident success is well-documented. Clance and Imes (1978) first identified the "impostor phenomenon," describing it as an internal experience of intellectual phoniness. This feeling often stems from unrealistic expectations and societal pressures, much like the ones I faced. I felt inadequate, especially in the medical field, surrounded by professionals who had been in their careers for decades. I felt like an impostor, constantly trying to prove myself with new certifications and higher education, yet always feeling like I was coming up short.

Then there were relationships. I've been married twice, divorced twice, and now I'm a solo mom of two amazing kids. It took years to appreciate that this was exactly how it was supposed to be. My first marriage was a trial run and a practice for adult life. Homeownership, career paths, and fidelity all crumbled under the weight of unhealthy behaviors and alcohol. We called it quits four short years in. The second marriage was more intense, and while I won't bore you with the details, let's just say I'm glad it ended. Those years taught me more about myself than I could have learned otherwise. Post-divorce, I've been having the time of my life because I finally realized how confining traditions can be. I had upheld the traditions offered to me in childhood, and they made me feel unworthy, questioning my very existence.

Once I understood that it was tradition, not truth, holding me back, I began to shift. One decision led to another, ultimately leading to my emotional, physical, and spiritual freedom. I was meant to have children with him, to relocate with him, but then start anew as a single mom shortly thereafter. It took years of slowly rebuilding, Recalibrating, and finally listening to my gut to regain my sense of worthiness.

Next, confronting the behaviors that sprouted from my core beliefs was a hell of a ride. For example, I realized that when I tried to adhere to the tradition of having a unilateral career, I felt like shit. I realized that I was always on a mission to prove my success, not just to others, but to myself. This mindset became so ingrained that facing myself in the mirror felt like a struggle. Trying to be the nicest, most approachable person around and sticking to what I thought was the accepted version of success left me feeling pretty damn unworthy most of the time. Compliments? I couldn't handle them. I was overly thankful for any kindness thrown my way and found myself apologizing for taking even a moment for myself. My dreams were kept locked away, hidden from others out of fear they'd judge or not believe in them.

RECALIBRATE YOUR SELF-WORTH

One of the most significant behaviors that sprouted from my core belief was that I had to play the part of a wife who was not involved with everyday financial decisions. As my marriage downward spiraled, I realized I had blurred the lines between fact and fiction in order to protect and uphold my core belief of traditional marriages. I created a narrative that overshadowed what was really happening, undermining my self-worth. The more I blurred reality, the shittier my interpretations became, stopping me from truly living. The following is an example of how I blurred the lines between fact and fiction and the impact it had on my reality.

The day I was handed that piece of paper, everything I thought I knew crumbled. We were being audited by the IRS for a "miscalculation" from years ago, and suddenly, we were staring down at an overwhelming amount of debt. My heart sank as I realized the enormity of the situation and the fictional story I had been telling myself for years prior. I thought I was being taken care of and that his decisions were of the best interests for both of us. I thought that we were a team and made decisions together. When I was told that he had known about this for several weeks, discussed it with a family member first, it was like a knife to the heart, a betrayal that left me reeling. To think he would share something of this caliber with anyone other than me felt like a haymaker to my face. I felt as though the foundation of our marriage had been built on lies instead of the bond of trust and teamwork. The façade of living a life as partners was exposed, and the evidence lay in the IRS document was harsh and unforgiving. The anger bubbled up inside me, not just at the financial mess we were in, but at the realization that the partnership I believed in was nothing more than a sham. I was not his confidant, rather, just one of the many pieces of his puzzle. I was left to pick up the pieces of a life that had been more illusion than reality, feeling utterly let down by someone I had trusted implicitly.

Looking back, I can see that the reality wasn't just about the debt. It was that I hadn't felt deep emotion in the relationship for years until that moment. I now understand that although this was a significant event, it allowed me to connect with the emotional void I had created in order to uphold the picture of a perfect marriage. The lies and stories I told myself had built walls around me, keeping me from experiencing genuine connections to my own life. As I started to uncover each subsequent lie or truth, I found myself feeling more deeply and authentically than I had in a long time. It was through this realization that I began to challenge how I created my reality based on my core beliefs of integrity, honesty, and trust rather than relying on a tradition.

Now, when I share something intimate, it's because I truly want it to be a part of me and the other person, not just because it's expected. This experience taught me a valuable lesson about the power of being true to myself and feeling my way through each day, rather than being on autopilot. We all create stories to shield ourselves from pain or vulnerability, but these stories often keep us from the real connections we crave. When I began to let go of these stories, I discovered a deeper connection with both myself and those around me.

By recognizing these patterns, I started rewriting my story. I began to understand that my worth wasn't tied to a single career path or conforming to what society expected. I learned to embrace new experiences, value my own company, and accept compliments without feeling like a fraud. This journey of self-discovery and redefining my core beliefs showed me the beauty in vulnerability and the strength in being real. Through this process, I finally started living life more fully, embracing the reality that I'm enough just as I fucking am.

RECALIBRATE YOUR SELF-WORTH

I encourage you to take a moment to reflect on your own life and try to separate your truths from the stories you tell yourself. Remember, you're not alone in this journey. Many of us struggle with the same challenges. The key difference is whether you're ready to embrace your truths or still feel the need to rationalize, explain, or hide them. Embracing authenticity can lead to a richer, more fulfilling life, where your relationships are built on genuine connections and sincere emotion. It's okay to take this journey at your own pace, knowing that each step toward honesty is a step toward deeper, more meaningful relationships.

The final step in this recalibration is stepping back into love with a genuine, forgiving perspective. Bring awareness to daily experiences that hold you back. Feel your way through decisions, from breakfast choices to choosing a partner. It is all about feeling your way versus thinking your way through. You're no longer bound by traditions or expectations that don't serve you.

Here's what helped me Recalibrate my story:

1. **Ease into your body.** Feel the sensations as you make decisions. When aligned with your true desires, you'll feel calm and confident. If it doesn't, you will likely feel on edge, short-tempered, and have physical discomfort. This aligns with Carver and Scheier's (2000) research on self-regulation and the importance of recalibrating personal goals to adaptively manage emotions and behavior.

2. **Observe your communication habits.** Notice when you interrupt, give advice, or react emotionally. Understanding your communication style helps you share opinions openly and honestly. It also helps us to understand our own hangups, perceptions, and beliefs. Wallace-Hadrill and Kamboj (2016) emphasize the role of cognitive reappraisal in emotional regulation,

highlighting how perspective changes can impact interpersonal interactions.

3. **Distinguish facts from fiction.** Avoid making assumptions about situations. Recognize when you're creating stories rather than observing facts. This is critical in maintaining a balanced perspective and avoiding the pitfalls of cognitive distortions, which can skew our perceptions of reality.

Working through handed-down traditions is crucial. You'll never reach your desired destination (recalibrating your self-worth) without appreciating how far you've come. As you examine how stories and traditions have shaped your life, you'll gain clarity and align with your true guidance system. Whether it's spirituality, religion, or science, find what resonates and supports you unconditionally as you break free from your past and embrace the person you were meant to be.

Ok, this chapter was about seeing, understanding and appreciating the mold that life's traditions and expectations have cast us in. Turns out, they were more like self-imposed constraints, but once recognized, they were the stepping stones to a life that felt real and no longer automated. I had to face the core beliefs and associated behaviors that were holding me back and learn to distinguish fact from fiction in the stories I told myself. By doing so, I started to rework my reality and let go of the traditions that no longer served me.

As we move forward, I invite you to explore your own beliefs and traditions. Let go of what doesn't serve you and embrace the freedom to create a life that aligns with your deepest values and aspirations. This is your journey, your story, so make it one worth telling. Now, let's take this newfound freedom and dive into a whole new beast: fear. Yeah, that's right, fear of both failing and succeeding. It's a mindfuck, really. Just when you think you've broken free, these fears creep in, trying to pull you back into old patterns. In Chapter 4, we kick off Phase 2 by exploring how shifting perspectives can lead to epic personal growth. We'll also meet a dear friend of mine, Andy. Through his story, you will see how he grappled with fear and redefined what success means to him. His story reminds us that while society might push us to chase achievements, real success comes from within. It's about aligning with your true self and kicking those fears to the curb. So buckle up, because we're about to embark on a journey that's as crucial as it is attainable. Time to Recalibrate and step into a life that's authentically yours.

Phase 2
Shifting
Perspectives

CHAPTER 4

The Fear of Failure and Success

"Only those who dare to fail greatly can ever achieve greatly."
Robert F. Kennedy

In the kaleidoscope of human experience, the fear of failure and success intertwines, creating a complex tapestry of emotions that often leaves us feeling paralyzed. This chapter delves into the depths of these fears, exploring how they shape our lives, decisions, and self-perception. Through Andy's story, we uncover the transformative power of recalibrating and can experience the journey toward self-acceptance.

Andy was a dancer who seemed to have it all. A talent that took him to stages around the world, a lifestyle many dream of, and a network of influential friends. His tall, lean frame and charismatic presence made him the center of attention wherever he went. But beneath the surface, Andy was struggling. His life, filled with applause and accolades, had become a gilded cage, trapping him in a cycle of success that no longer brought him joy.

It was a serious injury that forced Andy to pause and really look at his life. Lying in a hospital bed, surrounded by the monotonous beep of medical machines, Andy found himself confronted with a mix of fear, uncertainty, and surprisingly, relief. The injury, while painful, gave him a moment to breathe and a chance to stop the relentless chase for perfection and ask himself what he truly wanted. Recovery was tough. Each day was filled with therapy sessions that tested his patience and pushed his physical limits. But these sessions also gave Andy the space to reflect on his life. Faced with the fact that he could no longer be a professional dancer, he had to re-evaluate how he was going to make an income. He quickly realized that his life was a result of his income, not necessarily a result of what he valued. He began to question the importance of the material things he had accumulated like luxury cars, designer clothes, and a sprawling house because of his career choice. They had once seemed so important, but now felt trivial compared to the clarity he was beginning to find.

One day, Andy stood in his living room, surrounded by boxes of possessions he had collected over the years. Each item was a piece of his past, yet also a weight holding him back. As he let go of these things to pay his bills, he felt a sense of freedom and lightness. It was as though he was shedding an old skin, ready to embrace a new chapter of his life. As he healed, Andy turned to mindfulness and meditation, seeking peace amidst the chaos of his thoughts. Meditation became a daily practice, a time to quiet his mind and listen to what his heart was telling him. Through this, Andy learned to live in the moment, accepting his body's changes and embracing them as part of his journey.

During one of these meditative sessions, Andy experienced a profound sense of connection. He realized that his fear of failure and fear of not being enough were just shadows, not reality. With this understanding,

Andy began to redefine what success meant to him. It wasn't about wealth or fame anymore; it was about self-acceptance and finding worth within himself. This new perspective was redeeming. Andy found joy in teaching and mentoring young dancers, sharing not just his skills but his journey of self-discovery. Standing in front of eager students, he felt a fulfillment he had never known before. Teaching was no longer about perfection; it was about inspiring others to find their own paths.

Throughout his recovery, Andy was surrounded by a community of friends and family who supported him. They reminded him that he wasn't alone, and their belief in him helped him believe in himself. These relationships, based on genuine connection and understanding, became the foundation of his new life. Andy learned the power of vulnerability through these connections. By sharing his struggles, he found strength and a deeper connection with others. No longer afraid of sharing his perceived failure, Andy embraced the unknown with curiosity, exploring new opportunities and passions without hesitation.

Travel became a way for Andy to find inspiration and growth. He danced with traditional troupes in India and meditated in Bali's serene landscapes, discovering joy in the journey rather than the destination. These experiences taught him about the beauty of impermanence and the importance of living in the present. Reflecting on his journey, Andy realized that his story was one of transformation. He had moved from fear and uncertainty to a life filled with authenticity and fulfillment. His legacy wasn't about fame or fortune, but about inspiring and empowering others. Andy's story became a message of hope, encouraging others to embark on their own journeys of self-discovery.

In the end, Andy found some peace by living a life that truly matched his values and passions. His journey is a reminder that finding your authentic self is a tough-ass ride, but it's so worth it. For anyone stuck at a crossroads, Andy's story is pure inspiration, showing it's never too late to switch up your path and be your true self. His journey shows us the huge impact of living life aligned with what really matters to you, proving that authenticity brings real fulfillment. It takes courage to break away from what society expects and follow a path that truly resonates with your inner self.

This reflection naturally leads us to question the broader ideas of what success and happiness really mean. In the next chapter, we dive into these questions through Brianna's journey. Her story pushes us to rethink the usual success markers like money, career and relationships and invites us to dig into the deeper reasons behind our life choices.

CHAPTER 5

Reclaiming Self-Worth

"You are your best thing."
Toni Morrison

As we navigate the labyrinth of life, the quest for fulfillment often leads us to question the traditional pillars of success: finance, career, relationships, health, spirituality, and more. These elements, while important, can sometimes overshadow a more pressing inquiry: Why do we allow others' expectations to dictate our paths? This chapter explores the internal struggle of recalibrating one's life on personal terms and through the lens of Brianna, whose journey from self-doubt to self-discovery exemplifies the power of shifting perspective.

Brianna, a vibrant young professional in the healthcare industry, stands at a pivotal moment in her life. With striking blue eyes that seem to hold untold stories and a cascade of curly brown hair, she exudes a quiet strength that belies her turbulent past. Her journey is one of profound transformation, marked by the realization that her self-worth had long been tethered to the opinions of others.

RECLAIMING SELF-WORTH

Growing up in a small town where conformity was the norm, Brianna was the quintessential people pleaser. It was the kind of place where everyone knew each other's business, and stepping out of line was like painting a target on your back. Her slender frame and graceful demeanor were deceptive, concealing the inner turmoil that plagued her throughout her formative years. On the outside, Brianna was the perfect daughter, the perfect student, the perfect friend. But inside, she was a storm of insecurity and self-doubt.

In high school, Brianna's life was a balancing act, a tightrope walk between who she was and who she thought she needed to be. One of the ever-present internal battles Brianna faced daily was with her physical appearance and weight. Adhering to the perfect persona that was created, any deviation would send her into a tailspin. Control is what she thought she needed to ensure approval. So much so that she meticulously scheduled doctor's appointments in the morning, hoping the scale would reflect a lighter weight. Each visit was a ritual, a small act of control that masked a deeper insecurity. This constant comparison to her peers left her feeling inadequate. She was haunted by the whispers of her classmates, the subtle looks, the unspoken judgments. Every glance in the mirror was a reminder of what she wasn't, a silent scream of insufficiency.

College was supposed to be a fresh start, a chance to reinvent herself. But it brought new challenges that Brianna was unprepared for. Gaining weight after a knee injury was a devastating blow. It was like the universe had conspired against her, stripping away the fragile facade she had worked so hard to maintain. Trapped in a cycle of disordered eating and excessive exercise, Brianna's life spiraled out of control. Her days were dictated by calorie counts and workout schedules, her mind consumed by an obsession with food and body image.

Her mother's suggestion of a formal weight loss program was meant to help, but it only worsened the situation. What was intended as a lifeline became the gateway to an even deeper obsession. The program's rigid structure and relentless focus on numbers fed into Brianna's need for control, turning her life into a prison of self-imposed rules and restrictions. She was caught in a vicious cycle, a relentless pursuit of an unattainable ideal that left her exhausted and empty. The pressure to conform to societal standards of beauty was suffocating. Every magazine cover, every social media post, every casual comment about weight felt like a personal attack. Brianna's world was a battleground, her mind a war zone where every meal was a conflict, every reflection a confrontation. She was fighting a losing battle, and the toll it took on her mental health was devastating.

The breaking point came one cold, gray afternoon. Brianna sat alone in her dorm room, surrounded by the trappings of her meticulously curated life. The walls seemed to close in around her. The silence was deafening. It was as if the weight of her despair had finally become too much to bear. In that moment, she felt utterly alone, trapped in a body she despised, living a life that felt like a lie. It was then that Brianna made a desperate decision, one that would serve as a wake-up call. The suicide attempt was a cry for help, a last-ditch effort to escape the pain that had consumed her for so long. But it was also a turning point, a moment of clarity amidst the chaos. In the aftermath, as she lay in a sterile hospital room, Brianna realized that she had reached the end of a road she could no longer travel.

Admitted to an inpatient facility, Brianna was forced to confront the reality of her situation. The sterile walls of the hospital room mirrored the emptiness she felt inside. It was here, in this room devoid of any personal effects, that she faced her unraveling life. This was also the room where she met a therapist who would change the trajectory of her life.

This therapist, with her no-nonsense approach and empathetic heart, challenged Brianna to distinguish between what she needed and what she deserved. Brianna needed food and health; she deserved happiness and fulfillment. This distinction became the cornerstone of Brianna's recovery. Through countless therapy sessions, tears, and moments of raw honesty, she began to rebuild her life. She learned to appreciate her body not for its appearance but for its strength and resilience. Social media, once a source of validation, became a tool for empowerment as she shared her journey with others, inspiring them to embrace their authentic selves. Brianna's story is a testament to the power of ongoing contemporary psychological research in the importance of shifting perspective.

Studies emphasize the importance of intrinsic motivation and self-determination in achieving long-term well-being. When individuals make choices aligned with their values and desires, rather than external pressures, they experience greater satisfaction and fulfillment (Damen, van Amelsvoort, van der Wijst, & Krahmer, 2019). Experts in the field, such as Gaby Bernstein, Jay Shetty, Abraham Hicks, and Joe Dispenza, stress the role of self-compassion and mindfulness in recalibrating one's mindset. These practices encourage individuals to embrace their imperfections and view challenges as opportunities for growth. By shifting focus from external validation to internal fulfillment, individuals can break free from the cycle of self-doubt and achieve sustainable happiness (Wallace-Hadrill & Kamboj, 2016). Brianna's journey is not merely a story of recovery but of recalibration. Her transformation from a self-critical young woman to a confident, purposeful individual highlights the resilience of the human spirit. Each step forward was a victory, each setback a lesson, as she learned to navigate life on her terms.

This shift in perspective allowed Brianna to redefine success, not as an endpoint but as a continuous journey of self-discovery. By embracing her past and appreciating her present, she found the courage to pursue a future that resonated with her true self. Research shows that altering one's perspective can profoundly impact emotional well-being. For instance, shifting visual perspectives during autobiographical memory retrieval can influence emotional responses, suggesting that how we view our past can change how we feel about it (Küçüktaş & St Jacques, 2022). This cognitive flexibility is crucial for emotional resilience, personal growth, and recalibrating self-worth. When we remember an event that may have a negative connotation, it can impact our self-worth in the same fashion. However, based on the research if we are able to shift perspective around the same event, outline the positive aspects of the event and focus on those, we could shift how feel about it thus positively impacting our self-worth.

A study conducted by Damen et al. (2019) examined how explicit perception-focus instructions affect perspective-taking, revealing that such interventions can enhance empathy and understanding in interpersonal interactions. This aligns with Brianna's experience, where changing her perspective helped her connect more authentically with herself and others. Similarly, Wallace-Hadrill and Kamboj (2016) reviewed the impact of perspective change as a cognitive reappraisal strategy, finding it effective in reducing negative effects and increasing positive emotions. This emphasizes the importance of cognitive strategies in managing emotional health and aligning perceptions with personal values.

Brianna's story and the supporting research illustrate that shifting perspective is not merely a cognitive exercise but a transformative journey. By embracing this shift, individuals can move beyond societal expectations and rediscover their intrinsic value. This process is not without challenges, but as Brianna's story shows, the rewards of living authentically are profound. As we conclude this chapter, let Brianna's journey inspire a reevaluation of your own path. Ask yourself: Are you living in alignment with your true self, or are you bound by the expectations of others? The power to change your perspective and your life rests within you. Embrace it. As you reflect on your journey, consider this: What legacy do you want to leave, and how can you align your actions with your authentic self? By approaching life on your terms, you can unlock the potential for true fulfillment and growth. By redefining success on your terms, you can find empowerment and fulfillment, challenging you to question whose expectations you are really living for.

Alright, folks, we've tackled some heavy shit about perspective shifts and finding our true selves, but now it's time to crank it up a notch. We're diving headfirst into Chapter 6, where reality is more of an illusion than a solid ground. Ever felt like your life is just a series of social media stories strung together for likes and validation? Well, hold onto your seats because we're about to unravel that tightly wound facade. Meet Alex, the guy who thought he had it all figured out, only to realize his life was a curated showreel devoid of real meaning. As we explore the difference between curation and cultivation, get ready to question everything you thought you knew about living authentically. Let's take off the filters and embrace the raw, unfiltered truth of who we are and what we truly want.

CHAPTER 6

Your Life is an Illusion

*"There is nothing noble in being superior to your fellow man;
true nobility is being superior to your former self."*
Ernest Hemingway

In this chapter, we go into the concept of reality as shaped by the digital age; a reality that's more illusion than substance. Social media platforms like TikTok, Facebook, and Instagram have, in just two decades, woven themselves into the fabric of our daily lives, influencing everything from our food choices to our parenting styles. This chapter challenges you to discern between curation and cultivation in your life, which is a critical step in recalibrating your path to authenticity and worthiness.

Alex, a marketing executive in his mid-thirties, epitomizes the struggle between curation and cultivation. With a meticulously groomed beard and a wardrobe that screams sophistication, Alex is the kind of person whose Instagram feed looks like it could be in a magazine. His life seems perfect, a curated collection of filtered moments and hashtag-worthy experiences. But beneath this polished exterior lies a deep-seated dissatisfaction. Raised in a small town, Alex was always the overachiever, the kid who collected tributes and praise like they were going out of style. His parents, traditional to the core, instilled in him the belief that success was measured by societal approval. So, he curated his life with expensive suits, luxury vacations, and a social media presence that proved that he had "made it" to fit that mold. Yet, despite checking all the boxes, his relationships were mediocre at best, and Alex felt unfulfilled and somewhat bored.

The turning point came during a particularly sleepless night, one of those endless stretches of darkness where every minute seemed to drag on forever. Alex lay in bed, his eyes glued to the pale glow of his phone screen, which cast an eerie light across the room. His thumb moved mechanically, scrolling through endless feeds filled with seemingly perfect lives represented by smiling faces, exotic vacations, and beautifully plated meals. Each image felt like a taunt, a reminder of a world that seemed so effortlessly out of reach. Like most, he believed what he saw to be the truth. He turned to his own account, viewing the images.

As the hours ticked by, a growing sense of emptiness settled in his chest, a hollow ache that was becoming impossible to ignore. Each scroll deepened the void, leaving him feeling more isolated and disconnected. He realized, with a clarity that cut through the fog of his mind, that he wasn't living for himself anymore. His feed mimicked those of all the others. Just like the other accounts, his life had become a series of moments crafted for the approval of others, his worth measured in likes and comments. Then, out of nowhere, the truth hit him like a ton of bricks: So much of his life was a fucking illusion. Waiting for someone to call him out, to reveal how much untruth he kept. It was like a ticking time bomb, waiting to explode. The worst part was that he was responsible because he created it, one day at a time. It was a revelation that rocked him deep in the pit of his stomach, as if someone had ripped away a veil he'd been hiding behind for years. His existence was a carefully curated facade, a delicate shell lacking genuine meaning or fulfillment.

Alex sat there, stunned, feeling as if he were standing on the edge of a cliff, staring into the depths of his own soul. He was saddened about how much time he'd lost chasing after an illusion, sacrificing his own dreams for fleeting validation. In that moment of raw honesty, tears welled up in his eyes, exposing a mix of grief for the years wasted and relief at finally confronting the truth. For some reason, he felt relief. Relief that only comes to those who admit defeat and accept the truth. Relief that comes with acceptance of what was. Relief that no more lies must be told.

The path ahead was uncertain, but for the first time in a long time, Alex felt a flicker of hope. He realized he had the power to change, to break free from the chains of expectation and rediscover what truly mattered to him. With a deep breath, he set his phone aside, the screen finally going dark. It was time to begin the journey back to himself, one genuine, messy, beautiful step at a time.

Desperate for change, Alex began asking himself pivotal questions: Was he curating or cultivating his life? Were his possessions and experiences truly for him, or simply for show? This introspection led him to the stark realization that his life, while picturesque, lacked personal significance. Determined to forge a path of authenticity, Alex embarked on a journey of recalibration. Deleting the accounts was too much to handle so he made his accounts private. He started by decluttering his life, both physically and emotionally. Gone were the designer clothes that made him uncomfortable or fidget too much. He stopped returning the calls from the people he knew were just superficial relationships and began investing his time on the relationships that served him.

With each step, Alex began to cultivate a life rooted in personal meaning. He explored new hobbies, rekindled old friendships, and invested time in experiences that enriched his soul rather than his social media feed. This process wasn't easy; it required confronting uncomfortable truths and letting go of deeply ingrained habits. After about a year, Alex had the courage to delete his social media accounts because they no longer represented him and his interests. As a final testament to his transformation, he deleted the applications on his phone so he no longer compared himself to others. His self-worth came from intrinsic validation and no longer came from strangers.

Alex's journey is a microcosm of a broader societal issue. Research in both psychology and sociology discusses the impact of social media on self-perception and mental health. Studies reveal that the constant comparison to curated online personas can lead to feelings of inadequacy and anxiety (Hermann, Morgan, & Shanahan, 2021). Experts advocate for a shift toward cultivation and developing a life that aligns with personal values and passions rather than external expectations (Persohn, 2021). This shift involves embracing self-awareness and mindfulness, practices that encourage individuals to live in the present and appreciate their unique journey (Kathke, Tomann, & Uhlig, 2022). By focusing on intrinsic goals, such as personal growth and meaningful connections, individuals can break free from the cycle of temporal living and experience true fulfillment. Oh, and here's my personal recommendation: Put your fucking phone down. Engage with the people around you. Enjoy the coffee in silence. Relish the downtime that you have, and seriously, try to live life unplugged for a while.

Alex's transformation from curator to cultivator is a testament to the power of recalibration. His journey from the constraints of societal expectations to the freedom of living authentically brought a new sense of purpose, a deeper connection to himself and the world around him. As Alex learned to let go of curated living and embrace the flow of life, he discovered a profound sense of peace. He realized that true success isn't about what you have or how others perceive you; it's about living a life that resonates with your core values and brings you joy.

The rise of social media has significantly altered how we perceive ourselves and others. Social media platforms have become arenas for self-presentation and social comparison, encouraging users to craft idealized versions of their lives (Valenza, Boyer, & Curtis, 2014). This curation of life can lead to social media fatigue, where individuals feel overwhelmed by the need to maintain a certain image or keep up with others (Zheng & Ling, 2021). The curated nature of social media often leads to a disconnect between one's online persona and real life, creating an illusion that can be difficult to maintain. This disconnect can result in emotional distress, as individuals struggle to reconcile their true selves with the identity they present online (McLean, 2022). See how this can become a rabbit hole?

Cultivation, on the other hand, is about nurturing one's true self and focusing on personal development. It involves creating an environment that fosters growth and authenticity, rather than one that simply looks good from the outside. Cultivation requires introspection and a willingness to embrace vulnerability, allowing individuals to live in alignment with their values and passions (Persohn, 2021). The process of cultivation encourages individuals to engage in activities that bring genuine satisfaction and to form connections that are meaningful and fulfilling. This approach can lead to a more balanced and satisfying life, as individuals learn to prioritize what truly matters to them. Above all else, it feels fucking good, better than curation any day of the week. Alex's story is a powerful reminder that our lives are not meant to be illusions crafted for the approval of others. Instead, they should be authentic reflections of who we truly are and what we genuinely value. By recalibrating our paths and focusing on cultivation over curation, we can create lives that are rich with meaning and satisfaction.

As you reflect on your own journey, consider this: Are you living for yourself, or are you trapped in the illusion of societal expectations? Challenge yourself to embrace your authentic self, and let the answers guide you toward a life of fulfillment and growth. Alright, hang tight, because as we leave the illusion behind, we're diving into Chapter 7, Rising from the Ashes. Here's where we step into Phase 3, where daily recalibration becomes your new best friend using a tool to bridge the gap between the life you've lived and the one you're ready to lead. You will meet a force of nature who's at a crossroads, ready to redefine her existence. Her journey is all about confronting fears, embracing strengths, and refusing to be a prisoner of the past. Get ready to see how recalibration isn't just an idea; it's a revolution that can transform your life, one intentional step at a time.

Phase 3
Recalibration

CHAPTER 7

Rising from the Ashes

"Life tried to crush her,
but only succeeded in creating a diamond."
John Mark Green

Life is a series of recalibrations and moments when you must redefine who you are and what you stand for. This chapter delves into the journey of transformation, exploring the psyche of an individual who must confront her fears, motivations, strengths, and weaknesses to emerge stronger and more authentic. Through Ellen's story, we explore one way to navigate life's tumultuous waters to find true authenticity, purpose, and worthiness.

Ellen is an embodiment of flexibility. In her late thirties, she stands at a crossroads, her life a tapestry of diverse experiences with each thread representing a past role: HR specialist, alternative medicine practitioner, stay-at-home mom, and entrepreneur. Ellen is a woman of medium height, with striking hazel eyes that reflect her depth of thought and a cascade of auburn hair that symbolizes her fiery spirit. Her physical presence is both calming and commanding, a testament to her years as a professional.

Ellen's journey began in a small town where traditions were valued above all else. Raised in a family that prioritized maintaining the status quo, she learned early on the art of sacrificing her true self to keep peace. Her father's stern demeanor and her mother's quiet compliance taught her to suppress her desires, shaping her into a chameleon that could adapt to the expectations of others. However, beneath this facade lay a fierce yearning for authenticity and freedom.

Several years ago, Ellen was soaring. Her career as an entrepreneur was not just thriving; it was flourishing beyond her wildest dreams. She had worked tirelessly to build her company from the ground up, pouring her heart and soul into her business. She became a respected name in her industry, known for her innovative ideas and relentless drive. Her company was not just a business; it was a testament to her dedication and passion, representing years of hard work and sacrifice. This was the legacy she wanted to leave for her children, and she was damn proud.

Ellen's life seemed perfect from the outside. She had a loving husband, Mark, who she believed supported her endeavors, and two beautiful children who were the light of her life. She managed to juggle the demands of her career with her responsibilities at home, often working late into the night after putting her children to bed and rising early to prepare breakfast and pack lunches. Her life was a delicate balancing act, but Ellen was determined to make it work.

However, beneath the surface, tensions were brewing. Mark had always seemed to be supportive of Ellen's career, at least in the beginning. He would praise her accomplishments at social gatherings, boasting about her success to anyone who would listen. But as Ellen's career began to overshadow his own, a subtle shift occurred. Mark's pride slowly morphed into resentment. He started to feel like he was living in Ellen's shadow, his own achievements paling in comparison to her soaring success. Mark's resentment festered, manifesting in passive-aggressive comments and subtle jabs that Ellen initially brushed off. "Must be nice to come home to a clean house without lifting a finger," he'd say with a forced smile, or "I guess I'll handle the kids' school projects again this week." Ellen, caught up in the whirlwind of her career, missed the warning signs. She was too busy trying to maintain the precarious balance of her life to notice the growing chasm between her and Mark.

One evening, after a particularly grueling day at work, Ellen returned home to find Mark waiting for her in the living room, his face a storm of emotions. "We need to talk," he said, his voice tense. Ellen's heart sank. She knew this conversation was long overdue, but she wasn't prepared for the direction it would take. Mark accused her of neglecting their family, claiming that her career had become her sole focus. "You're never here, Ellen," he said, his voice rising. "You're always at work or thinking about work. What about us? What about the kids?" His words hit Ellen like a punch to the gut. She had always prided herself on being able to juggle her responsibilities, but now, faced with Mark's accusations, she began to doubt herself.

Mark's words were like poison, and that is all it took. The seeds were planted and seeping into Ellen's mind, sowing seeds of self-doubt. She started to question her choices, wondering if she had indeed neglected her family in her pursuit of success. Every time she stayed late at the office or took a business call at home, Mark's accusations echoed in her mind, turning her accomplishments into a source of guilt and shame. The situation only worsened as Mark began to weaponize Ellen's career against her in more insidious ways. He started to use it as a tool to undermine her confidence, belittling her achievements and suggesting that her success was not truly her own. "You're only doing well because you're a woman in a male-dominated field," he'd say dismissively, or, "Your success is just a fluke. It won't last."

Ellen's self-doubt grew, fueled by Mark's constant barrage of criticism. She began to second-guess herself at work, hesitating before making decisions that she would have confidently made before. Her performance suffered, and with it, her sense of self-worth. The vibrant, confident woman who had built a successful company was slowly being eroded, replaced by someone who questioned her every move. Mark's manipulation extended beyond their private conversations. At social gatherings, he would make snide remarks about Ellen's work, cloaked in the guise of humor. "Ellen's the boss at work," he'd say with a smirk, "but at home, she's just another mom who cleans up the floors on her hands and knees." Laughter would follow, but Ellen felt the sting of his words keenly, each comment chipping away at her self-esteem.

Despite the turmoil at home, Ellen tried to maintain a brave face at work. She threw herself into her projects, hoping that her passion and dedication would be enough to silence the doubts in her mind. But Mark's words lingered, a constant reminder of her perceived failures as a wife and mother. Her work, once a source of pride and joy, became a battleground, a place where she fought to prove herself worthy. The breaking point came during a family dinner, when Mark openly criticized Ellen in front of their children. "Your mother's too busy at work and that is more important than spending time with us," he said, his tone dripping with disdain. Ellen's heart broke as she saw the confusion and hurt in her children's eyes. As time passed, she worked in silence, never sharing achievements or struggles with anyone, let alone Mark.

The rejection of her keynote talk at a prestigious college was the final blow in a series of emotional upheavals. When the rejection letter arrived, it felt as if the ground opened beneath her and swallowed any ounce of worthiness she had left. The letter, with its formal language and impersonal tone, seemed to echo her husband's criticisms, amplifying her fears that perhaps she had indeed lost her way. The words blurred as tears filled her eyes, each sentence feeling like a confirmation of her deepest insecurities. Ellen was engulfed by a wave of self-doubt and fear. She felt like a stranger in her own life, questioning her worth and direction. "Who am I now if I am no longer this person? What good am I to anyone?" and "He was right all along." Her voice was meek, and her cheeks were stained with tears while these questions haunted her, echoing in the quiet moments of solitude and in the bustling noise of her daily life.

Ellen had found herself in a place darker than she ever imagined possible. Life had thrown her into a pit of despair, where every day felt like trudging through mud. She was overwhelmed, stressed, and tired of the relentless cycle of shit that seemed to keep coming her way. There were moments when she felt like she was drowning in a sea of hopelessness, with nothing but the shadows of her own fears and doubts to keep her company. It was during these bleak days that Ellen realized she needed to make a change, not just for herself, but for her children. They were the light in her life, the reason she got up every morning, even when all she wanted to do was pull the covers over her head and shut out the world. She knew she had to dig deep and find some sort of resilience to keep moving forward, no matter how small that scrap might be.

At first, it was just a tiny spark of independence that began to glow inside her. It was like a single match in the darkness, and it didn't seem like much at all. But Ellen clung to it, nurturing that little flame with every ounce of strength she could muster. She understood that endurance wasn't going to come from some dramatic, life-changing event. Instead, it would grow from the small, deliberate choices she made every day.

Ellen started by taking a long, hard look at herself. She began to reflect on her life, examining the things that had brought her to this point. It wasn't easy; introspection rarely is. She realized that she had been carrying around a lot of shit that wasn't hers to bear, and it was time to let it go. The baggage was his, not hers. With each passing day, Ellen made a deliberate choice to shift her perspective. Owning what was hers, releasing the projected negativity he imposed on her. She rejected his tainted memories and versions of his reality and viewed life from her own lens. Finally. She began to focus on the things she could control, rather than being consumed by the chaos that surrounded her. She started separating herself from him, knowing the challenges it carried, but the benefits outweighed the regret. This took determination, grit, and perseverance. It took every ounce of strength because at every good fortune and upward turn she experienced, he lurked and attempted to destroy her efforts. She started setting small, achievable goals for herself, celebrating each victory, no matter how insignificant it might seem. Quietly and without his knowledge, she added fuel to that spark of independence, helping it grow stronger and brighter.

Ellen leaned on the support of her friends and family. She opened up about her struggles, something she had been reluctant to do in the past. Sharing her burden made it feel lighter, and the encouragement and love she received in return were invaluable. Her children, with their unyielding belief in her and their unconditional love, became her greatest source of inspiration. She wanted to show them that even in the darkest times, it was possible to rise up and fight back.

She also turned to prayer, seeking solace and grounding in her faith. It was in these moments of quiet reflection that she began to rebuild her confidence, piece by piece. Through groups, she discovered new approaches, innovative strategies that reignited her passion and reminded her of her capabilities. Through her relationships, she unearthed a network of support that she had previously overlooked. Friends and mentors rallied around her, offering encouragement and perspective, helping her to see herself through their eyes. Slowly but surely, Ellen began to reassemble the fragments of her identity.

Little by little, Ellen began to see changes in herself. She was more patient, more present, and more hopeful. The independence she had worked so hard to cultivate was becoming a part of her, shaping her into someone stronger and more determined. She was no longer just surviving; she was living, with a renewed sense of purpose and a fierce desire to create a better life for herself and her children. She emerged from this period of introspection stronger, wiser, and more determined than ever. The rejection, once a symbol of her perceived failure, transformed into a catalyst for growth. It taught her that setbacks are not the end, but rather a part of the journey toward self-discovery and fulfillment. She had made a deliberate choice to fight for herself and her family, and in doing so, she had found independence she never knew she had. Ellen's story is a reminder that even in the darkest moments, there is always a flicker of hope waiting to be ignited.

Ellen's path to rebuilding was neither straightforward nor easy. It was a dance of two steps forward, one step back. Yet, she learned to embrace the fluidity of life. In less than one year, she achieved what seemed impossible, landing an invite to a series of keynote speaking events, which further propelled her career. This success was not just external; it reflected her internal transformation. Ellen's journey of recalibration was marked by a profound shift in perspective. She learned to hang out with experience, allowing herself the pleasure of being amazed and then changed. This transition from the past was not just an emotional release but a strategic recalibration of her life's compass.

Ellen embraced new experiences, learning to savor moments of wonder and change, which helped her transition from her past and welcome a future full of possibilities. By pairing her dreams with a transformative determination, she mobilized her intentions in a focused and organized manner, creating a personal mantra: "I can, I will, and here is the reason why." Her desire to live authentically and experience happiness and satisfaction fueled her journey, bringing her to a state of sound mind and true freedom. Committed to realizing her intentions, Ellen made significant life changes, such as leaving toxic relationships, relocating, taking breaks, finding new jobs, and inviting fresh experiences into her life.

Ellen's journey is another testament to the power of recalibration. She teaches us that we will never get to where we want to be until we appreciate how far we have come. Her story is an example for those lost in the shadows of other people's judgment, a reminder that authenticity and freedom lie just beyond the fire and ashes of transformation. So, just as Ellen's fiery journey of recalibration teaches us to rise from the ashes, Chapter 8 takes us on a wild ride with Shane, who's navigating the tricky terrain between worthiness and success. If Ellen's story was about finding her true self amidst judgment, Shane's tale is about redefining success on his own terms. Get ready to dig into Shane's world, where the pressure to fit a mold is relentless, but the urge to break free is even stronger. It's time to explore how embracing authenticity can bridge the gap between feeling worthy and achieving real, satisfying success by shattering old paradigms and building a life that truly aligns with who you are.

CHAPTER 8

The Bridge Between Worthiness and Success

"Our deepest fear is not that we are inadequate.
Our deepest fear is that we are powerful beyond measure.
It is our light, not our darkness, that most frightens us.
We ask ourselves,
'Who am I to be brilliant, gorgeous, talented, fabulous?'
Actually, who are you not to be? You are a child of God.
Your playing small does not serve the world."
Marianne Williamson

In this chapter, we explore the delicate balance between feeling worthy and achieving success. It's a journey that involves recalibrating our internal compass to align with our true values and aspirations. This is the story of Shane, a character whose life exemplifies the struggle and triumph of finding this balance.

Shane is in his mid-forties when he shared this story. A successful entrepreneur who built a thriving business from the ground up, he stood tall with an athletic build (courtesy of his past as a collegiate athlete),

Shane exudes confidence. His sharp blue eyes often seem to pierce through façades, revealing a deep understanding of human nature. Yet, beneath this exterior lies a history marked by self-doubt and the relentless pursuit of external validation. Raised in a conservative family, Shane was taught that success equated to adherence to tradition. His parents, both highly successful in their fields, instilled in Shane the belief that worthiness was tied to achievement and societal approval. This upbringing led Shane to sacrifice his true self to fit into a mold he never truly identified with. The pressure to succeed was immense, leaving little room for self-discovery and authenticity. Fast forward a few decades.

Shane sat at the edge of the hotel bed, the city lights flickering outside the window like distant stars, a stark contrast to the darkness that had settled in his chest. The interview had been a whirlwind, a testament to years of hard work, yet as the journalist's final question lingered in the air. "What does success mean to you?" A silence had followed, deep and unsettling. Shane had always been quick with answers, a master of articulating strategies and achievements, but this time, words failed them. Suddenly, the honors, the awards, and the relentless pursuit of excellence all felt like an elaborate lie. The realization was both a whisper and a roar: none of it had been for him. It was as though Shane had been running a marathon without ever knowing why, only to find himself at the finish line feeling more lost than ever.

In the days that followed, Shane found himself trapped in a fog of confusion. The once-clear path of ambition was now obscured by questions that seemed to have no answers. *Who am I without my success? What do I truly want?* These thoughts were relentless, echoing in the quiet moments between meetings and during sleepless nights. The vacuum of certainty left Shane feeling hollow, like a shell of his former self. He had been so consumed by the chase that he had never paused to understand what he was actually chasing or why, for that matter. The emptiness was overwhelming, a vast expanse of uncertainty that threatened to swallow him whole.

Shane began to withdraw from the world, skipping social events and avoiding the very people who had always praised his accomplishments. Each encounter felt like a reminder of the identity he had built on shaky foundations. Friends noticed the change, but Shane couldn't bring himself to explain. How could he articulate the profound sense of loss for something that had never truly existed? This was a turning point, albeit an uncomfortable one. For the first time, Shane faced the fear that had been lurking beneath the surface: the fear of not knowing who he was beyond his resume. The journey into self-discovery was daunting, filled with the weight of unexamined dreams and neglected passions.

Shane sought refuge in solitude, spending hours walking through the city, hoping the rhythm of his footsteps might somehow lead him to answers. He read voraciously, searching for stories of others who had walked this path, clinging to the hope that he was not alone in his struggle. As the days turned into weeks, a subtle shift began to take place. The vulnerability that had once felt like a burden started to feel like a strange, new kind of freedom. Shane realized that the emptiness was not a void to be feared but a space waiting to be filled with something authentic.

Though the path ahead was still unclear, Shane understood that this was a journey worth taking. It was time to discover what truly mattered to him, to build a life that resonated with who he was. It was terrifying, yes, but it was also an invitation to find meaning beyond the resume. In that uncertainty, Shane found a promise of new beginnings, of a life where success was defined not by external validation but by inner fulfillment.

The journey was just beginning, and for the first time, Shane felt a flicker of excitement about the unknown.

The recalibration process for Shane began with a critical step: turning inward. Stepping off the relentless track of achievement, Shane focused on self-awareness with his creative outlets. The practices of writing, drawing and sculpting allowed him to confront his past in private. The same emotions that had been shaping his decisions revealed patterns such as the fear of failure and the compulsion to please others. By asking himself, "What do I feel right now?" Shane gained clarity on his internal landscape.

Next, Shane began identifying his true values, such as freedom, ongoing creativity, and connection. These values became a new compass guiding his decisions. Through self-reflection, Shane was able to prioritize actions that aligned with these core values, making choices that resonated with his authentic self. Research by Rosi et al. (2019) supports the idea that aligning actions with personal values significantly enhances self-esteem and emotional well-being.

Redefining boundaries was another crucial step for Shane. He learned that pleasing others often compromised his own happiness. By asking, "How do I protect myself from external influence?" Shane began to take pride in his efforts, focusing on what he could control: his perspective and response. This approach is echoed in Carucci's (2023) discussion on personal growth, which emphasizes that success without personal boundaries often leads to dissatisfaction.

Inspired by the Buddha's Eightfold Path, Shane worked on aligning his actions with his values. He consistently asked, "Does this align with who I want to be?" ensuring a congruence between his values and his daily activities. This alignment is crucial, as suggested by Muñoz et al. (2023), who emphasize that maintaining self-worth in entrepreneurial ventures requires aligning personal and professional actions with core values. To master focus, Shane stopped multitasking and dedicated time to meditation and completing one task a time. He began concentrating on three key tasks each day, creating a routine that fostered both productivity and peace of mind.

Finally, Shane embraced a broader mindset by asking, "What am I holding onto, and what is the emotional weight of these thoughts?" This shift allowed him to release limiting beliefs and concentrate on growth, both personally and within his community. Carucci (2023) discusses how broadening one's mindset can lead to significant personal transformation, highlighting the importance of letting go of limiting beliefs to achieve true satisfaction.

Research into shifting perspectives and the sacrifice of self for tradition reveals that many individuals struggle with the dichotomy of maintaining societal expectations and pursuing personal fulfillment. Academic papers, books, and expert opinions highlight the importance of self-awareness and mindfulness in achieving a balance between worthiness and success. Trusted publications emphasize that daily practices of recalibration, such as meditation and reflection, are crucial for sustained satisfaction and success. Muñoz et al. (2023) provide compelling evidence that the deterioration of self-worth is a significant issue in entrepreneurship, often exacerbated by societal pressures and the pursuit of external validation. Similarly, Rosi et al. (2019) demonstrate the impact of failures and successes on self-esteem, emphasizing the importance of aligning personal values with professional actions to maintain emotional well-being. Carucci (2023) reinforces these findings by arguing that personal growth and transformation are essential for achieving true satisfaction, beyond mere success.

THE BRIDGE BETWEEN WORTHINESS AND SUCCESS

By integrating these types of insights, Shane's journey becomes a testament to the transformative power of self-awareness, value alignment, and the courage to redefine success on one's own terms. Through his story, you are encouraged to embark on your own path of self-discovery, bridging the gap between worthiness and success. Shane's journey is a powerful testament to the transformative power of self-discovery and recalibration. As we roll into Chapter 9, I will share how this book has been a tool for me and how it can be for you as well. How each chapter has been a deep dive into the heart of self-acceptance and the courage it takes to redefine what the hell it means to truly value yourself. It's time to explore how recalibrating self-worth can transform not just how you see yourself, but how you live your life.

CHAPTER 9

Recalibrating Self-Worth: My Story

"Seek to be whole, not perfect."
Oprah

As the sun dipped below the horizon, casting a warm glow over my cluttered makeshift desk, I took a deep breath and closed my laptop. The room was bathed in the soft, amber light of dusk, the kind that makes everything seem a little more magical, a little more hopeful. I had just finished reading the final edits of the stories and the research I had collected for this book, along with the final draft. A profound sense of relief washed over me as I realized the journey I embarked on over the last several months was finally coming full circle. This wasn't just about the words on the page, but about the transformation they had sparked within me. This journey began with an introspective look at my past and had led to a deeper understanding of my self-worth.

As I sat there, putting the final touches on my manuscript, I was filled with a profound sense of fulfillment and clarity. Writing this book has been an incredible journey, one that has mirrored and impacted my life in ways I never could have imagined. My life, much like the stories I've shared, is a tapestry woven with threads of triumph and heartache, each experience a testament to my own adaptability and resilience. I've ridden the roller coaster of life, experiencing the dizzying heights of professional success and the gut-wrenching lows of personal defeat. Yet, it was in the quiet moments of reflection, often alone in my modest home, that I began to see the patterns emerging. It was here that I started to Recalibrate again, to sift through the noise and find my own voice that had been drowned out by the cacophony of expectations and traditions I felt compelled to uphold.

My space, a small but cozy space, filled with mismatched furniture and piles of my kiddo's artwork, became my sanctuary. It was here, amidst the semi-organized chaos, that I began to piece together the fragments of my identity. Days spent curled up on the couch with my laptop, fueled by endless cups of coffee and the occasional frustrated outburst, became my norm. The process was anything but linear. There were days when the words flowed effortlessly, and others when I stared at a blank screen, paralyzed by self-doubt and the "Who the fuck will care about what I am writing?" moments. Writing this book was not just about overcoming self-doubt and ego; it was about the courage to shift very broad perspectives, to break free from the bondage of self-imposed limitations and external expectations. It was about sacrificing the false ego to embrace the true one. The journey fraught with fear but rich with the promise of self-discovery and self-worth. Through this process, I learned that aligning self-worth with compassion and sincere self-expression is essential for personal growth and truly becoming a master of my own life.

In researching for my book, I delved deeply into the works of psychologists, philosophers, and spiritual leaders. I explored insights on vulnerability, growth mindset, and Buddhist teachings on mindfulness and presence. Each book, each article, added a layer of understanding, helping me piece together a comprehensive view of self-worth and its intrinsic link to personal and professional fulfillment. The integration of these diverse perspectives was crucial in forming a holistic understanding of self-worth. The theme of recalibration resonates deeply with me because it taps into a universal truth: the need to redefine success on one's own terms. For many, the path to self-worth begins with the simple yet profound act of acceptance of where they are, what they have accomplished, and who they have become. It's about acknowledging both the light and the shadow within oneself and using that awareness to navigate forward. This concept is echoed in studies that highlight the impact of self-worth perception on achievement motivation, emphasizing the role of self-awareness in driving personal success.

This book includes anecdotes and personal stories that illustrate the transformative power of recalibrating self-worth. These narratives shared throughout the book are not just inspiring but also serve as practical examples of navigating the complex interplay between self-worth and societal expectations. It emphasizes the importance of accepting one's current state and how they got there, as the initial step in recalibrating self-worth. This involves honest reflection on achievements, failures, and the lessons learned from each past experience.

Mindfulness and presence, drawn from Buddhist teachings, play a significant role in cultivating self-awareness. By practicing mindfulness, individuals become more attuned to their thoughts and emotions, allowing them to make conscious choices that align with their true selves. Mindfulness practices can activate brain areas associated with self-related processing, reinforcing positive self-worth. Adopting a growth mindset is essential for embracing challenges and viewing failures as opportunities for learning and growth. I've found that cultivating a growth mindset helps me navigate setbacks with resilience and optimism, ultimately enhancing my self-worth. Individuals with a positive perception of self-worth are more motivated to achieve their goals. I encourage you to redefine success on your own terms, shifting away from societal or familial benchmarks and focusing on personal fulfillment. This involves setting goals that are meaningful and aligned with one's values, rather than those imposed by external pressures. Aligning self-worth with personal values is crucial for achieving true fulfillment. Finally, building resilience is a key component of recalibrating self-worth, enabling individuals to bounce back from adversity and maintain a positive outlook. This doesn't mean sticking your head in the sand nor does it mean thinking everything is rainbows and unicorns. Having a positive outlook means that although there is a negative aspect in each event, there is always a positive one. Acknowledge the negative, however focus on the positive one and sooner than later, you will begin to see more positives than negatives. I shared stories of people who faced significant challenges yet emerged stronger and more self-assured, emphasizing the importance of perseverance and adaptability.

As I write the final words of this book, I feel a sense of closure. I have come to understand that the bridge between worthiness and success is not built overnight. It reinforced what I knew all along. Bridging my past life with my current life requires daily acts of recalibration, moments of introspection that call to authenticity. My journey, along with the insights gleaned from the research and other peoples stories, offers you a roadmap for navigating your own path to worthiness and fulfillment. This book isn't just about sharing stories; it is a shout for those lost in the noise of expectations. It is about finding the courage to redefine what truly matters and not letting the world's noise drown out your own voice.

RECALIBRATE YOUR SELF-WORTH

The transformations are a testament that anyone can rise from the ashes of doubt and emerge with a life that's both authentic and fulfilling. It started with a deep dive into my own insecurities, removing layers of self-doubt and fear that had built up over the years. There were moments when I felt like I was standing on the edge of a cliff, staring into an abyss of uncertainty. But with each revelation, each step forward, I felt a little lighter, a little freer. The stories I shared became a mirror, reflecting my own struggles and triumphs, showing me the strength I had always possessed but never fully acknowledged. In the quiet solitude, I found solace in the stories of others who had walked similar paths. Their resilience, their courage, and their unwavering determination to live authentically inspired me to push forward. I realized that I was not alone, that my struggles were not unique, and that there was immense power in vulnerability.

You know, life's a real bitch sometimes. It throws you curveballs when you're least expecting them, knocks you flat on your ass, and leaves you wondering what the hell just happened. But through it all, there's this undeniable strength that bubbles up from somewhere deep inside, pushing you to get back up and keep fighting. That's resilience, right there, and it's about being able to strip away all the bullshit to get to what really matters.

CHAPTER 10

Embracing the Journey of Recalibration

"You are the master of your destiny.
You can influence, direct, and control your own environment.
You can make your life what you want it to be."
Napoleon Hill

As we stand together at the threshold of this final chapter, let's take a moment to breathe. Inhale deeply and feel the air fill your lungs. This is a simple act, yet it's a reminder of life's inherent rhythm that you are a part of. As you exhale, let go of the doubts and fears that have clung to you like shadows. This book has been your companion, a guide through the intricate dance of personal growth and recalibration. But now, it's your turn to take the lead.

Change is a word that often evokes a mix of excitement and fear. It's the unknown calling, whispering promises of new beginnings and uncharted paths. Yet, it's also a reminder that you must leave behind the comfort of the familiar when it no longer serves you. But here's the truth: Staying stagnant is not living; it's merely existing. You're not meant to live in the shadows of your potential. You're meant to shine, to explore the vast landscape of your capabilities and desires.

This book is more than just a collection of stories; it's a powerful invitation to Recalibrate your life. To step off the well-trodden path paved by societal norms and into the uncharted territory of your own making. You're invited to evaluate and then shift your perspective, to see the world not as it is, but as it could be through the lens of your dreams and aspirations. The stories shared are not just tales of triumph; they're blueprints for transformation. Each character faced their own demons, battled self-doubt, and emerged as stronger, more authentic versions of themselves. They are living proof that you, too, have the power to rewrite your narrative. Remember, there are three phases in recalibrating self-worth.

Phase One: Awakening from Autopilot

Alright, so you're here because you're tired of living a life that feels scripted by someone else. The first step to waking the fuck up is recognizing that you're on autopilot. This isn't some woo-woo shit; it's about taking a hard look at your life and asking, "Am I living intentionally, or just reacting to whatever life throws at me?" The kick in the ass often comes in many forms. Maybe it's a job that's sucking the soul out of you, or a health scare that makes you rethink your shitty habits. Maybe it's a broken relationship, or the overarching feeling that nothing is going your way. Whatever it is, it's your chance to hit pause and reevaluate what the hell you're doing with your life.

Unearthing the layers of your unconscious habits isn't easy. It's like ripping off a Band-Aid; it might sting, but it's necessary. Start by observing your daily routines and note the things you do without thinking. Are they energizing you, or do they leave you feeling like a zombie? Keeping a record of things you do and how you feel afterwards can help here. Write down what feels automatic and what genuinely brings you joy. It's a simple practice, but it's a powerful way to get to the heart of what really matters to you. Remember, you don't have to overhaul your life overnight. Start small. Maybe it's as simple as swapping your morning donut for a walk in the park or shutting your phone off at 7 PM. These tiny changes can have a big impact over time, helping you break free from the mindless cycle of autopilot living.

Mindfulness is your secret weapon. It's about being present and aware, so you can make conscious choices instead of just reacting. This awareness helps you align your actions with your true self, including your values, passions, and dreams. So, as you embark on this journey, know that it's uniquely yours. There's no right way to do it, and you're bound to stumble. When you do, be kind to yourself. Celebrate your progress, no matter how small, because each step forward is a step toward living a life that's authentically yours. Trust the process and keep moving forward.

Phase Two: Shifting Perspectives

You've taken the first step and woken the hell up from autopilot. Now it's time to tackle Phase Two: Shifting Perspectives. This is where we dive deep into the shit that's been holding you back, like those limiting beliefs that have been lurking in the shadows, fucking with your head and keeping you stuck in a rut. It's time to shine a light on them and show them the door.

First off, let's remember what limiting beliefs really are. They're the stories you tell yourself that say you're not good enough, smart enough, or whatever enough. They're the little fuckers that whisper, "You can't do that," or "You'll never succeed," or "You will look like an idiot." These beliefs are often shaped by our past experiences or people in your life and the bullshit we've absorbed from society. And man, do they run deep. To shift your perspective, you've got to start by recognizing these beliefs for what they are: lies. They're untruths, but they're not set in stone. They're just thoughts, and thoughts can be changed. So, how do you spot them? Pay attention to the self-doubt and fear that creep up when you're faced with a challenge. Notice the fixed mindset that says change is impossible. That's your cue to start digging deeper.

Once you've identified these limiting beliefs, it's time to flip the script. Enter: shifting perspective. This is all about looking at your situation from a new angle and finding the silver lining. So, you fucked up? Big deal. Instead of beating yourself up, ask, "What can I learn from this?" Every setback is a setup for a comeback. It's not failure; it's feedback. Let's say you didn't get that promotion you were gunning for. Instead of spiraling into a pit of despair, reframe it. Maybe this is the universe's way of telling you there's something better out there. Or maybe it's a nudge to develop a skill you've been neglecting. Reframing helps you see the bigger picture and opens up new possibilities you might have missed. If your limiting beliefs manifest in behaviors or coping mechanisms that you have been practicing for decades, it's ok to go back to the root of your belief. Just don't stay there. Acknowledge it and move forward. This is the crux of your journey and where recalibrating your self-worth is the bridge from your previous self to the person you want to be.

Now, let's get into focusing on what is actually working in your life versus all the shitty things that are not serving you. This isn't just some fluffy, feel-good shit. It's about rewiring your brain to focus on what's possible. Start by challenging the negative chatter in your head. When you catch yourself thinking, "I can't do this," counter it with the other side of the story, "What part of this is reasonable?" Shift and use phrases like "How can I approach this differently?" or "What is the bigger picture or message here?" and my personal favorites, "What am I ready for if this is what I am getting?" and "Today, I get to do this." Repeat questions like these until they become second nature. Focusing on the bigger picture and the positive aspects helps you build resilience and a growth mindset. You start to believe in your ability to handle whatever life throws your way. And that, my friend, is fucking powerful.

As you shift your perspectives, you'll start to see challenges not as insurmountable obstacles but as opportunities for growth. This isn't just about putting on rose-colored glasses and pretending everything's sunshine and roses. It's about recognizing the potential for learning and growth in every situation. When you embrace uncertainty and change, you open yourself up to a world of possibilities. Sure, it's scary as hell at first. But remember, the magic happens outside your comfort zone.

Here are some practical tools and exercises to help you shift your perspective that you can start using today:

1. **Journaling for Clarity.** Write down your limiting beliefs and challenge them. Ask yourself, "Is this really true?" "Is this even my belief?" and "What evidence do I have to support this belief?" This exercise helps you see your thoughts for what they are and begin the process of letting go.

2. **Visualization.** Spend a few minutes each day visualizing your ideal life. Imagine yourself living in alignment with your values and passions. Feel the emotions associated with this reality. I like to go even smaller. What does my next interaction look like? Visualization helps reinforce positive beliefs and keeps you focused on your goals.

3. **Appreciation Practice.** Start an appreciation journal and write down three things you appreciate each day. Focusing on the positive aspects of your life helps shift your perspective from lack to abundance.

4. **Mindfulness Meditation.** Practice mindfulness to stay present and aware. This helps you catch negative thoughts before they spiral out of control. Mindfulness also enhances your ability to reframe situations and approach them with a fresh perspective.

Shifting your perspective is a game-changer when recalibrating your self-worth. It's about breaking free from the chains of limiting beliefs and stepping into a life of possibility and growth. This phase of your journey requires commitment and courage, but the rewards are worth it. By challenging the narratives that have held you back, you open the door to a life that's aligned with your true self. Embrace this shift with an open heart and mind. Trust the process and know that every step you take brings you closer to the life you're meant to live. You've got the tools, the stories, and the community to support you.

Phase Three: Daily Recalibration

Welcome to Phase Three of your journey toward intentional living: Daily Recalibration. This is where the rubber meets the road, where you take all the insights and shifts you've experienced and weave them into the fabric of your everyday life. This phase is about creating a daily practice that keeps you grounded, aligned, and moving forward with intention.

Let's start with meditation, one of the most powerful tools for daily recalibration. I know what you're thinking. Meditation can seem like some mystical practice reserved for monks on mountaintops, but it's really just about finding a moment of stillness amidst the chaos. By setting aside time each day to meditate, you create space for yourself. This is your time to hit pause, breathe, and reconnect with your inner self. Meditation allows you to quiet the noise of the outside world, which, let's be honest, is usually a cluster of distractions and demands. In this space of stillness, you can foster a deeper understanding of your thoughts and emotions. Start with just a few minutes a day. Find a comfortable spot, close your eyes, and focus on your breath. As thoughts arise (and they will because your brain is a chatterbox), acknowledge them and gently return your focus to your breath. Over time, this practice cultivates a sense of inner peace and clarity that permeates your daily life.

Next up is reflection, an essential component of daily recalibration. This is your opportunity to take stock of where you are, where you've been, and where you're headed. Reflection is like looking in the mirror not just to see your reflection, but to understand it. Set aside some time each day, maybe in the evening, to reflect on your experiences. Ask yourself questions like: What went well today? What challenges did I face? How did I respond to them? What can I learn from this? How is this in alignment with the greater good and my long-term success? Reflection helps you gain insights into your progress and identify areas for improvement, enabling you to make future decisions that are aligned with your values and goals, ensuring that your actions are consistent with your intentions. Journaling or transcribing your reflection can be a powerful tools for this type of work. Write down or dictate your thoughts and feelings, and don't hold back. This is your space to be brutally honest with yourself. Over time, you'll notice patterns and insights emerging from your reflections, guiding you on your path of growth.

Once you've meditated and reflected, it's time to take intentional action. This is about making conscious choices that align with your values and aspirations. It's not about running on autopilot or doing things out of obligation. It's about setting clear goals and taking deliberate steps toward achieving them. Start by identifying your core values that truly matter to you. Is it creativity, family, adventure, or something else? Whatever it is, let these values guide your decisions and actions. When faced with a choice, ask yourself: Does this align with my values? Does it bring me closer to my goals? If the answer is no, it might be time to reassess and Recalibrate. Intentional action also involves prioritizing activities that support your growth and well-being. It's about saying fuck no to the bullshit that doesn't serve you and hell yes to the things that do. This might mean setting boundaries, delegating tasks, or simply taking time for yourself.

As you integrate these practices into your daily life, you'll begin to experience a sense of fulfillment and purpose. You'll learn to live in alignment with your values, making choices that honor your true self. This process of daily recalibration is not a one-time event but an ongoing journey. It requires commitment and dedication, but the rewards are well worth it.

Here's how you can start integrating these practices into your daily routine:

1. **Morning Meditation.** Begin your day with a short meditation session. This sets a positive tone for the day and helps you start with clarity and focus.

2. **Midday Check-In.** Take a moment halfway through your day to pause and check in with yourself. How are you feeling? Are you staying true to your intentions? This quick recalibration can keep you aligned and centered.

3. **Evening Reflection.** Spend a few minutes each evening reflecting on your day. What did you learn? What are you grateful for? This practice helps you process your experiences and prepare for the next day.

4. **Weekly Review.** Dedicate some time each week to review your progress and set intentions for the coming week. This bigger-picture reflection helps you stay on track and make necessary adjustments.

5. **Goal Setting.** Regularly revisit your goals and aspirations. Are they still aligned with your values? Are you making progress? Adjust as needed to ensure you're moving in the right direction.

Remember, daily recalibration is a journey, not a destination. There will be days when you feel aligned and on top of the world, and days when everything feels like a dumpster fire. That's okay. The important thing is to keep showing up, keep recalibrating, and keep your awareness up. Trust in the process and know that each step you take brings you closer to living a life of authenticity and fulfillment. You have the tools, the insights, and the determination to make it happen.

It's okay to feel scared or hesitant. Change can be overwhelming, and the unknown often looms like a shadow, casting doubt and fear. But consider this moment a gentle nudge from the universe telling you it's time to take that leap of faith. Imagine standing on the edge of a vast canyon, the ground solid beneath your feet, yet the other side promising new horizons. Your heart races, and your mind is a whirlwind of what-ifs. It's perfectly natural to feel this way. Fear is a powerful force, but it doesn't have to be paralyzing. Instead, let it be the fire in your belly that drives you forward.

EMBRACING THE JOURNEY OF RECALIBRATION

You are not alone in this journey. Each step you take toward self-discovery is a step that countless others have taken before you and will take after you. It's a shared experience, a collective endeavor where each of us inspires and uplifts the other. By sharing your journey, you not only empower yourself but also those around you. Your story, your struggles, and your triumphs become an example of hope for others navigating their own paths. As you continue to explore the depths of your own story, may you find the strength to rise above the constant chatter of expectations and doubt and listen to the whispers of your heart. Trust your instincts, for they are the compass guiding you toward your true north. And in those moments of doubt, remember to extend grace to yourself. You are a work in progress, beautifully flawed and wonderfully complex.

Recalibrating self-worth is about making a conscious choice every day once you have connected who you were and where you want to be. It's about choosing authenticity over conformity, purpose over comfort, and courage over fear. It's about understanding that true empowerment doesn't come from what you achieve, but from who you become in the process. The world is full of noise, telling you who you should be, what you should do, and how you should live. But none of that matters if it doesn't align with who you truly are. Embrace your quirks, your passions, and your dreams. Let them guide you in crafting a life that is uniquely yours. A life that is a testament to your resilience, your courage, and your unyielding spirit.

Finally, know that you are part of a collective. This collective is made up of individuals who are also on their journey of recalibration. Reach out, connect, and share your experiences. Together, we can create a world where authenticity is celebrated, where self-worth is not determined by external validation, but by the love and respect we have for ourselves. As we close this chapter, know that this is not the end, but rather the beginning of a new adventure. Your journey awaits, filled with endless possibilities and boundless potential. Embrace it with open arms, for it is a journey worth taking.

About the Author

Jen Traverse is a multi-faceted author, speaker, and nurse who shares her inspirational journey of self-transformation in her bestselling book series "Recalibrate."

After years spent pleasing others and feeling lost in the grind of daily life, Jen began to question if there was more out there for her. Through practices like meditation, she was able to let go of her fears and limitations to embrace a life of fulfillment, coincidences, and self-awareness.

In the "Recalibrate" series, Jen candidly shares her own experiences overcoming addiction, eating disorders, and transformational personal growth. With pragmatic examples and vulnerable storytelling, she provides readers with a framework to identify their fears, shift perspectives, and take aligned action to live a more authentic life true to themselves.

Jen appeals to diverse audiences, from overwhelmed moms to overworked executives, who resonate with her message of courage, empowerment, and tools for continual self-improvement. She aims to inspire others to Recalibrate their own lives by building spiritual practices like meditation, setting boundaries, and seeking community support.

With her warm yet candid approach, Jen encourages people to let go of expectations, transform fears into faith, and embrace their journey of self-discovery. Through her books, speaking engagements, and nursing practice, she hopes to inspire others to live their most fulfilling lives.

References

Carucci, R. (2023, January 25). Personal growth and transformation: Why success doesn't lead to satisfaction. *Harvard Business Review*.

Carver, C. S., & Scheier, M. F. (2000). Scaling back goals and recalibration of the affect system are processes in normal adaptive self-regulation: Understanding 'response shift' phenomena. *Social Science & Medicine, 50*(12), 1715-1722. https://doi.org/10.1016/S0277-9536(99)00412-8

Cascio, C. N., O'Donnell, M. B., Tinney, F. J., Lieberman, M. D., Taylor, S. E., Strecher, V. J., & Falk, E. B. (2016). Self-affirmation activates brain systems associated with self-related processing and reward and is reinforced by future orientation. *Social Cognitive and Affective Neuroscience, 11*(4), 621-629. https://doi.org/10.1093/scan/nsv136

Clance, P. R., & Imes, S. A. (1978). The imposter phenomenon in high achieving women: Dynamics and therapeutic intervention. *Psychotherapy: Theory, Research & Practice*, 15(3), 241–247. https://doi.org/10.1037/h0086006

REFERENCES

Creswell JD. Mindfulness Interventions. Annu Rev Psychol. 2017 Jan 3;68:491-516. doi: 10.1146/annurev-psych-042716-051139. Epub 2016 Sep 28. PMID: 27687118

Damen, D., van Amelsvoort, M., van der Wijst, P., & Krahmer, E. (2019). Changing views: The effect of explicit perception-focus instructions on perspective-taking. *Journal of Cognitive Psychology, 31*(3), 353–369. https://doi.org/10.1080/20445911.2019.1606000

Deci, E. L., & Ryan, R. M. (2000). The "what" and "why" of goal pursuits: Human needs and the self-determination of behavior. *Psychological Inquiry, 11*(4), 227-268. https://doi.org/10.1207/S15327965PLI1104_01

Fahd, S., Khurram, F., Akhtar, K., Siddique, U., & Javed, F. (2021). Impact of self-worth perception on achievement motivation among university students. *Journal of Management Practices, Humanities and Social Sciences, 5*(2). https://doi.org/10.33152/jmphss-5.2.3

Gouraud, J., Delorme, A., & Berberian, B. (2017). Autopilot, mind wandering, and the out of the loop performance problem. *Frontiers in Neuroscience, 11*, 541. https://doi.org/10.3389/fnins.2017.00541

Hermann, E., Morgan, M., & Shanahan, J. (2021). Television, continuity, and change: A meta-analysis of five decades of cultivation research. *Journal of Communication, 71*, 515–544. https://doi.org/10.1093/joc/jqab014

Holt-Lunstad J, Smith TB, Layton JB. Social relationships and mortality risk: a meta-analytic review. PLoS Med. 2010 Jul 27;7(7):e1000316. doi: 10.1371/journal.pmed.1000316. PMID: 20668659; PMCID: PMC2910600.

Joseph, R. (2022). A cross-sectional study of the relationship between self-worth and self-determination: Implications for social work ethics. *International Journal of Social Work Values and Ethics, 19*(3), 108-131. https://doi.org/10.55521/10-019-308

Kathke, T., Tomann, J., & Uhlig, M. (2022). Curation as a social practice: Counter-narratives in public space. *International Public History, 5*(2), 71-79. https://doi.org/10.1515/iph-2022-2046

Korponay, C. (2023). Snapping out of autopilot: Overriding habits in real time and the role of ventrolateral prefrontal cortex. *Perspectives on Psychological Science, 18*(2), 482-490. https://doi.org/10.1177/17456916221120033

Küçüktaş, S., & St Jacques, P. L. (2022). How shifting visual perspective during autobiographical memory retrieval influences emotion: A change in retrieval orientation. *Frontiers in Human Neuroscience, 16*, 928583. https://doi.org/10.3389/fnhum.2022.928583

Markus, H. R., & Kitayama, S. (1991). Culture and the self: Implications for cognition, emotion, and motivation. *Psychological Review, 98*(2), 224-253. https://doi.org/10.1037/0033-295X.98.2.224

McLean, A. M. (2022). Content creation vs. curation: Strategies for theological library social media coordinators. In *Proceedings of the Seventy-sixth Annual Conference of Atla*. Pitts Theology Library, Emory University.

REFERENCES

Muñoz, P., Barton, M., Braun, S., Chowdhury, F., Jayne-Little, N., Rowland, J., Sykes, K., Smith, J., Talbot-Jones, C., Taggart, A., & Komes, J. (2023). The deterioration of self-worth in entrepreneurship. *Journal of Business Venturing Insights, 20*, e00430. https://doi.org/10.1016/j.jbvi.2023.e00430

Pennebaker, J. W., & Seagal, J. D. (1999). Forming a story: The health benefits of narrative. Journal of Clinical Psychology, 55(10), 1243–1254. https://doi.org/10.1002/(SICI)1097-4679(199910)55:10<1243::AID-JCLP6>3.0.CO;2-N

Persohn, L. (2021). Curation as methodology. *Qualitative Research, 21*(1), 20-41. https://doi.org/10.1177/1468794120922144

Rosi, A., Cavallini, E., Gamboz, N., Vecchi, T., Van Vugt, F. T., & Russo, R. (2019). The impact of failures and successes on affect and self-esteem in young and older adults. *Frontiers in Psychology, 10*, 1795. https://doi.org/10.3389/fpsyg.2019.01795

Ryan, R. M., & Deci, E. L. (2000). Self-determination theory and the facilitation of intrinsic motivation, social development, and well-being. *American Psychologist, 55*(1), 68-78. https://doi.org/10.1037/0003-066X.55.1.68

Siddiquee, M. S. A. (2024, September 29). The power of deliberate thinking: Escaping autopilot and taking control of your mind. *Medium*. Retrieved from https://medium.com/@msa.sid/the-power-of-deliberate-thinking-escaping-autopilot-and-taking-control-of-your-mind-31e3574c0e3a

Tedeschi, R. G., & Calhoun, L. G. (2004). Posttraumatic growth: Conceptual foundations and empirical evidence. *Psychological Inquiry, 15*(1), 1-18. https://doi.org/10.1207/s15327965pli1501_01

Traverse, J. (2023). *Recalibrate your fear: Transform your fear into safety.* [Paperback edition].

Traverse, J. (2022, May 17). *Why asking for help is your superpower* [Video]. TEDxClintonMiddleSchool. https://www.youtube.com/watch?v=R0jP8SYGXsQ

Valenza, J. K., Boyer, B. L., & Curtis, D. (2014). Social media curation. *Library Technology Reports, 50*(7). http://ebookcentral.proquest.com/lib/emory/detail.action?docID=1883992

Wallace-Hadrill, S. M., & Kamboj, S. K. (2016). The impact of perspective change as a cognitive reappraisal strategy on affect: A systematic review. *Frontiers in Psychology, 7*, 1715. https://doi.org/10.3389/fpsyg.2016.01715

Wirtz, J. (2020). *Recalibrate (Black & White Edition).* Independent Publisher.

Wirtz, J. (2021). *Recalibrate - The Workbook.* [Paperback edition].

Zheng, H., & Ling, R. (2021). Drivers of social media fatigue: A systematic review. Library & Information Science Abstracts, 64(November). http://www.proquest.com/lisa/docview/2593195782/6261A3EC9C0B4B28PQ/12?accountid=10747